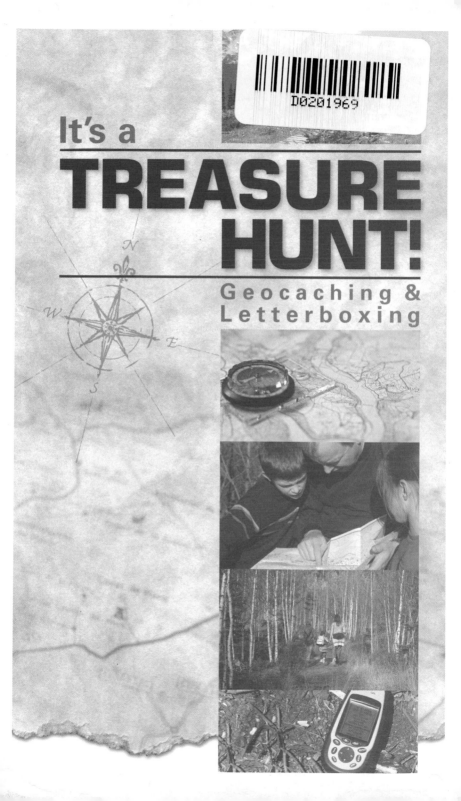

It's a
TREASURE
HUNT!

Geocaching &
Letterboxing

Printed in the United States of America
by G&R Publishing Co.

Distributed By:

CQ Products

507 Industrial Street
Waverly, IA 50677

ISBN-13: 978-1-56383-268-0
ISBN-10: 1-56383-268-2
Item #7025

Table of Contents

Geocaching and letterboxing are two exciting, new pastimes for adventure-loving people! They are high-tech versions of hide-and-seek that combine the thrill of scavenger hunts, the physical challenges of hiking, and the fun of gift exchanges while using a hand-held global positioning system receiver (GPSr) or compass.

Whether searching for geocaches filled with trinkets to exchange, or seeking out letterboxes containing special rubber stamps to use, the satisfaction is in the hunt itself. It's a perfect activity for families to enjoy together, either in their local area or while traveling on vacation. All you need is computer access and an accurate GPS receiver or compass.

This book explains all the basics... and also includes pages that are perfect for preserving the priceless memories you'll create together. Start now!

What is
GEOCACHING?

Players use a global positioning system receiver (GPS or GPS receiver) to find a cache, then sign the logbook and exchange small trinkets.

Geocache

jē′ ō: having to do with the earth's geography

kăsh: a hiding place for provisions; a safe place of
concealment for valuables; a store of goods in
a cache

A geocache is a small waterproof container filled
with interesting trinkets, a logbook and a pencil. It has been
carefully packed and hidden in some out-of-the way spot
in nature with the hope that outdoor enthusiasts will follow
special clues to hunt for it. It's a scavenger hunt for treasure
that's begging to be found – and geocaching is the wildly
popular game people are playing in order to find it.

But geocaching isn't an ordinary scavenger hunt. What
sets it apart is the use of technology: a handheld GPS receiver
(global positioning system). The player who hides a cache
pays special attention to exactly where s/he has hidden it and
then records its location on a GPS receiver. After s/he gives
online clues on special websites, other players can hunt for this
hidden treasure and report their finds.

The clues?
Latitude and longitude coordinates on
the GPS receiver plus some hints.

The method?
Use of your GPS receiver plus deciphering
cryptic clues to guide you to the correct
location of the hidden treasure.

The challenge?
To actually find the treasure which is well-
hidden between rocks, under dry brush, in
trees or inside caves.

The payoff?
The fun of the hunt and the satisfaction of
uncovering a hidden treasure, plus maybe
an exchange of trinkets.

History of Geocaching

Satellites orbit the earth 12,500 miles above us to act as a navigational system for space exploration and military operations. But ordinary civilians can use this technology today by using a hand-held global positioning system receiver. For people on the ground, the GPS receiver collects signals from at least 4 different satellites, takes measurements and then automatically computes the location of the person holding the receiver. The readings on a GPS receiver are listed as degrees of latitude and longitude. The receiver can also calculate altitude and distances. Although receivers aren't perfect, they can generally guide you to within 10 or 20 feet of the treasure, depending on your location and the quality of the GPSr.

Signal Reception

Weather does not affect a GPS receiver enough to hinder geocaching. You should still get a good signal in rain, snow or cloudy weather. However, if you are near tall buildings, in a valley or under a cover of trees, especially pine trees or those that are rain-drenched, your signal may be distorted or weak. If you are driving in a car in the rain, your windshield wipers may also affect your signals.

As GPS receivers became less expensive and more accurate, and as people became more technologically savvy, new hobbies were bound to appear. In May 2000, clear channels became available to the general public so readings became much more accurate. As a result, the sport or game of geocaching was born.

Geocaching started as a way for technology fans to have a little fun. Dave Ulmer, the '"father of geocaching", hid a sealed 5-gallon bucket with a logbook, some small trinkets and money tucked inside. He used his GPSr to record the latitude and longitude coordinates of the bucket's hiding spot, shared that information with his online newsgroup and encouraged other GPS users to go on a treasure hunt to find the bucket.

Ulmer also encouraged people to hide and share their own caches. He specified just one "rule": Finders should take something from the treasure and then leave something else behind for the next hunter.

Within a week, others in his newsgroup had hidden and posted new caches in California, Illinois and even Australia. After finding a cache, the treasure hunters wrote about their experiences online. Before long, a website was launched to collect all these interesting tales and tips in a single place that the public could read. This emerging new hobby was called geocaching, and its popularity is growing quickly.

Today there are hundreds of thousands of caches hidden in more than 200 countries worldwide. Now you can join the fun too! Just follow the seven easy steps beginning on page 9.

Guiding Principles of Geocaching

Geocaching is treasure hunting with a moral compass as well as a physical one. The guiding principles of the sport include concern for the environment, valuing physical activity and leaving places better than they were found, which includes picking up trash along the way. If you plan to go geocaching, it's important to follow these principles, from the Geocachers' Creed, in both hunting and hiding caches.

1. I will not endanger myself or others.
2. I will observe all laws and rules of the area.
3. I will respect property rights and seek permission where appropriate.
4. I will avoid causing disruptions or public alarm.
5. I will minimize my and others' impact on the environment.
6. I will be considerate of others.
7. I will protect the integrity of the game pieces.

The complete Geocachers' Creed can be found online at www.geocreed.info.

Geocaching How-Tos
7 Easy Steps

1

Gather your geocaching supplies

- GPS receiver
- Pen or pencil
- Internet access
- Nickname (or username)
- Trinkets (optional)

Choose a reliable GPS receiver in your price range after doing some research in a sporting goods store or online. You may wish to borrow or rent receivers first to see which features you like best. (See "Buying a GPS receiver" below.) Carry your own pen or pencil to sign the logbook inside the cache in case the one provided isn't functional.

You'll need Internet access to visit websites that list geocaches hidden in your hunting area. After reading about them, you can choose the ones you wish to find. One good website to use is www.geocaching.com.

You will also need to choose a nickname for yourself or your group. Make it silly or memorable, and use it to sign the logbooks when you find caches. This nickname can also be your username for the geocaching websites.

Buying a GPS receiver (GPSr)

There are many basic GPS receivers available today. A simple one is all you need for geocaching. Choose one that is easy to hold and use, durable, waterproof and has good features for a reasonable price. Be sure the print shows up clearly on the screen. The buttons should be plainly marked and well-placed so you won't push them unintentionally. It's smart to buy one with a data cable so you can enter coordinates via the computer. A built-in compass feature is handy but not a necessity if you have a reliable magnetic compass available. Look for clear and concise operation instructions!

One good way to research receivers is to read the message boards on different geocaching websites to see what other people recommend.

Families who want to collect small treasures from a cache will want to bring some interesting trinkets or small items to trade and leave in the cache. Some people like to keep track of all their finds and trinket exchanges. Use the logbook pages in this book (or a small notebook) to record the details and dates of each cache you have hunted for and your results.

Two optional tools may make your hunt easier: a reliable magnetic compass and topographic maps for the areas you wish to hunt. But these items are not needed for simple family excursions along well-marked trails.

Pack your hiking supplies

Before going on a hike of any sort, pack a few essentials. A small backpack or fanny pack is a good way to carry everything. Take along a small flashlight, gloves, tissues and spare batteries* for your GPSr in a zippered plastic bag. It's also a good idea to take a plastic bag along to collect any trash you find.

Since geocaching is an outdoor adventure, it's also wise to pack items like bandages, sunscreen, bug repellant, water and high-energy snacks. If young children are hiking with you, bring other items as needed to make their experience enjoyable and safe. Hiking boots and walking sticks may be helpful for people of all ages when the terrain is uneven.

Types of Caches

Traditional Caches
This icon* indicates a traditional cache.

Before you go hunting, it's nice to know what you are looking for. People hide a wide variety of caches, but most are packed in hard, waterproof containers like army surplus ammunitions cans, plastic food storage containers or buckets with tight-fitting lids. The items inside the container will usually be enclosed in heavy-duty plastic baggies that zip. Since

*Battery Tips

GPS receivers run on batteries. Alkaline batteries are easy to find and reasonably priced. They will last for about 12 operating hours in a GPS receiver. Rechargeable batteries generally don't last as long but can be recharged many times. Lithium batteries are expensive but will run your receiver for 30 or more hours.

To conserve battery power, turn off the receiver when you aren't using it, for example, after you have found the cache. (Watch the icon on your GPS screen to monitor your battery power. If you see that your batteries are running low, replace them before starting a hunt.)

Cold Climates

Geocaching in winter can be a great activity. Your GPS receiver will be very accurate since there is little or no leafy tree cover. You won't have a bug problem either. But a few extra supplies will make your hunt safer, such as a cell phone, cold weather clothing including a hat, scarf and gloves, extra dry socks, a thermos holding a warm drink and perhaps chemical hand warmers. Pay extra attention to weather reports and use good common sense.

Types of Caches

geocaches are hidden outdoors and need to withstand all types of weather, the containers must protect the trinkets inside from damage. That's not to say that they can't be washed away in flood waters or dragged away by a hungry animal!

The trinkets hidden inside caches can vary from practical things like batteries, bug repellant packets or a mini-compass, to kid-friendly items like stickers, action figures, whistles or other small toys. Some caches even contain items with monetary value, like pro-sports tickets, gift certificates, state quarters or silver dollars.

3

Choose a cache to find

Go online to a geocaching website, sign in and set up an account using your chosen nickname. Then type in the country, state or zip code of the area you'd like to visit for geocaching. All the hidden geocaches that fit your information will be listed. You can choose one or more of these caches for which to hunt based on difficulty, terrain rating, clues and/or the description of the cache and its location.

If you're a beginner, it's best to choose caches that are easy to find and indicate they have been found recently. Reading the logs of recent visits written by people who have found the cache within the past few days almost ensures the cache is still there and hasn't been stolen or washed away in a heavy rain.

Beginners or those with young children may also want to choose caches that involve shorter hikes on relatively flat terrains or well-marked trails, allowing strollers or bicycles to be used. If you don't want to tread through thick underbrush, look for caches hidden in plain sight in areas with little overgrowth.

Traditional caches also vary in size. Some are as large as a five gallon bucket. An average size cache would be a plastic food container or ammo can that holds at least one quart. A small cache would be more like the size of a sandwich container, holding less than one quart.

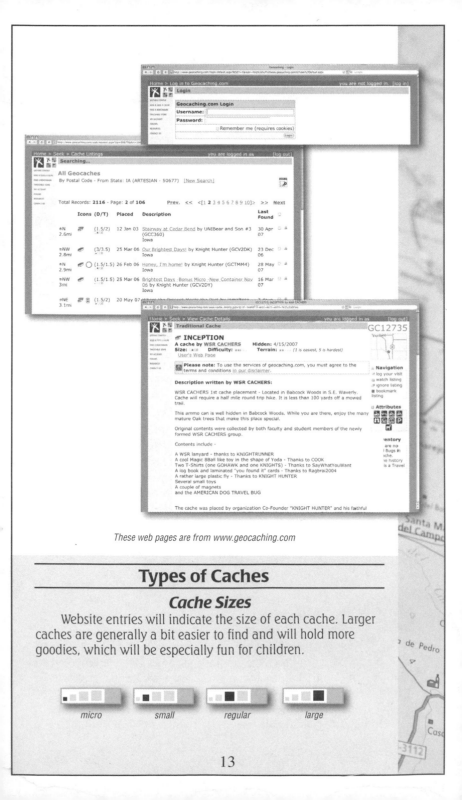

These web pages are from www.geocaching.com

Types of Caches

Cache Sizes

Website entries will indicate the size of each cache. Larger caches are generally a bit easier to find and will hold more goodies, which will be especially fun for children.

micro   small   regular   large

4 Load your GPS receiver

Follow the instructions on your own receiver to enter the latitude and longitude coordinates of each cache you wish to find. Label each pair of coordinates (a waypoint) with a different name. It's smart to print off a copy of the website page with the information about each cache, and then take it with you on your hike. This information might have clues to decode or additional cryptic hints to help you find the cache if you get stuck. You may want to print a second copy to leave in your vehicle so others know where you are in case of emergency.

If you must drive your vehicle and park a distance from the cache's hiding place, enter the latitude and longitude of your vehicle's parking spot as a waypoint labeled CAR. (You can also enter and name other junctions or landmarks as waypoints along your path as you pass them.) The car waypoint will help you find your vehicle again when you are finished hiking.

There will be several ways to search with your GPSr. Use the map display on the GPSr screen and follow the arrow to begin your hike. Watch the distance display too. As you get closer to the cache, you may wish to zoom in on your map to see more details. You may instead choose to follow the built-in compass in the "go to" function. It will also point you toward the treasure.

Types of Caches

Microcaches

In the country or open areas, it isn't too difficult to find good hiding spots for larger traditional caches. But what about urban areas? In order to be sure the hidden treasures aren't easily discovered or taken by non-geocachers, it's often necessary to make very small caches. The smaller they are, the more challenging they can be to find. A mint or pill box, plastic 35mm film can, plastic bead box or other airtight container

14

GPS Reminders

Before beginning your hike, be sure your receiver is set on the correct "map datum system". WGS 84 is commonly used for geocaching. (Older maps often used a NAD 27 system.) Your receiver's instructions will explain how to check this.

When you turn on your GPS receiver, it takes a few minutes to lock into the satellites. After it does, the latitude and longitude display on the screen will be your current location. In order to find a cache, you must enter the coordinates for the place you wish to go and label those as a named waypoint. Then the GPSr is able to plot a route from your current location to the waypoint where the cache is hidden. (Cache coordinates are listed on websites.)

Use the map display on your GPS receiver and follow the arrow to the cache. Or, use the "go to" feature and follow the built-in compass.

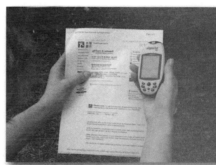

Types of Caches

that's tiny can be hidden so that only those who know what they're looking for will find it.

That doesn't allow much space for trinkets, but there should still be paper inside to use as a logbook and record finds. A strip of cash register tape may work well for the logbook. If you're lucky, a tiny pencil might be included inside, but when hunting for micros, it's a good idea to bring your own pencil to sign the logbook.

continued on page 18

Coordinates

Latitude lines run horizontally around the globe and are parallel to the equator. (Clue: lat = flat.) These lines measure the distance north or south of the equator. (They will be your north/south coordinates.)

Longitude lines run vertically on the globe between the North and South Poles. (Clue: long = long lines.) These lines measure the distance east or west of the prime meridian in Greenwich, England. (They will be your east/west coordinates.)

For GPS activities, latitude and longitude coordinates will usually show up on your display as a number, measured in degrees (°) and decimal minutes without seconds. The latitude coordinate will include a north or south direction. The longitude coordinate will include an east or west direction. A cache will be hidden where these two coordinates intersect.

Information on your GPS could look like this, including the elevation:

N42° 44.557
W092° 30.164
Elevation 953 Ft.
This example means the location of the cache is north of the equator by approximately 42 degrees, 44.557 minutes and west of Greenwich, England by 92 degrees, 30.164 minutes. Since 1° latitude is about 69 miles, the cache location in this example is a little more than 2,898 miles north of the equator (42 degrees x 69 miles). But fortunately, you don't have to figure out distances; your GPS receiver can calculate them correctly and you just need to use the coordinates!

(If you followed the coordinates above, they would take you to CQ Products in Waverly, Iowa. Stop in and say hi!)

Geocaching Jargon

Signature item – A personalized trinket that a geocacher leaves in a cache almost every time s/he finds one, such as a special patch, pin, or metal or wood coin. It could include a signature card that other geocachers collect like trading cards.

Hitchhikers – A trinket with instructions to be moved. This trinket is supposed to be taken and then moved into a different cache of your choice in another area, city or state. You give it a ride to another location. There is often a logbook with it to record the hitchhiker's travels.

Travel bugs – One type of hitchhiker that has a special tag with an assigned tracking number obtained online. The travel bug's journeys can be followed on the website as each finder writes an online entry about the experience.

Spoilers – Information posted on a website about finding a cache that gives too much away, thus "spoiling" the hunt for others. (A spoiler can be a person or the information itself.)

Stash – Another name for a treasure or cache. The first treasure hunt with GPS receivers was called "The Great American GPS Stash Hunt", but today the common name has been changed to geocaching.

Swag – A name for the trinkets traded in a cache.

Geocoin – A small personalized metal coin that may be left as a trinket or signature item in a cache. Wooden nickels can also be ordered online and personalized for trading as a signature item. Official USA Geocoins can be tracked online, like travel bugs.

Waypoint – A pair of latitude and longitude coordinates that identifies a place on earth. Cache locations are waypoints, but so are other spots you choose to save, name, store and recall on your GPS receiver, such as your vehicle's parking spot!

Muggles or Geomuggles – Similar to the muggles from the Harry Potter books, geocaching muggles refer to people in the general public who are not geocachers. They may stumble upon a hidden treasure and never realize what it is, or they may report suspicious activity if they see geocachers hiding or seeking a cache! Beware of muggles. Do your hunting and hiding secretively.

5 Start your hunt!

You have chosen a cache to find, loaded your GPS receiver with the coordinates and packed all your supplies. Now it's time to start your hunt. The GPS receiver will lead the way using the map display or compass display from the "go to" feature. Just hold it in front of you and follow the arrow on the screen. Stay on the trail for as long as you can, but when the arrow points in another direction, you will probably have to leave the trail to find the cache.

As you get closer, perhaps within 30 feet or so, slow down and pay very close attention to all the details around you. You can't rely on the GPS completely at this point because it will not take you directly to your treasure. It's time to use your eagle eyes and your detective skills to search for the best hiding spots. Is there a good hiding spot near the roots or in the branches of that tree? Could that fallen log hold a cache?

Types of Caches

Sometimes micros give clues to find another, larger cache. Sometimes these tiny caches are attached to metal objects with magnets. They might also be tucked into hollow objects that look like part of the urban landscaping such as a plastic rock in a rock garden or a green tube tucked into a hedge.

Why is the grass flattened in a path toward that rock? What's that white thing under the bush?

Pay attention to the way things look. Remember that the cache owner will try to disguise the cache in many ways including camouflage duct tape, paint and nature's own cover. You may need to approach the area from different directions, working in a cloverleaf pattern around your GPS coordinates.

Other Hunting Tips

- A topographic map may help you avoid or move around unexpected obstacles such as steep ridges, streams or even buildings. (Follow a link from the cache listing to find a topographic map of the area near the cache, then print it and take it along on your hunt.)

- Remember that distance and direction on your GPS receiver are measured in straight lines or "as the crow flies". If you have turns and hills, your hike can be longer.

- As you get closer, it may be time to pull on gloves to protect your hands in case you are in an area with prickly bushes, sticky pine branches or a muddy terrain.

- Remember to be somewhat secretive during your hunt to avoid giving away the hiding spot to other potential geocachers or calling undue attention to your activity.

Types of Caches

Tips for finding Micros

Look in spots other than eye-level, where most people tend to look.

- Look **behind** metal surfaces such as road signs.
- Look **under** objects such as park benches.
- Look **up** into trees, in branches, squirrel holes or abandoned nests off season.
- Look **among** natural objects, like rocks. You might find a fake hollow rock which holds the treasure.

6 Your find!

You've ducked under low-hanging branches, stepped over muddy streams and picked cockleburs off your jeans. You've crawled through underbrush, searched under rocks and peered into hollow tree stumps – and you finally found it!

Now what do you do? The first thing is to observe and remember exactly how the cache was hidden, its position and how it was disguised. Being observant will help you put it back the way you found it. Then, do what any good treasure-hunter does: Step away from nearby people, open the cache, look at the things inside and read the logbook to see who else has successfully found this treasure before you.

If there are trinkets inside for taking, help yourself to an item and leave something else of equal or greater value in its place (a basic rule of geocaching). If there's a camera inside, you may take your picture and put the camera back. However, be aware that if you do not want your picture posted on a website, you shouldn't take your photo.

Sign the logbook with your nickname and write down the date and time of your find and what you've taken or left. Include a "thank you" or other positive comments about the hunt, the site or the cache. Messages are usually brief, but sometimes wannabe writers or comedians include short jokes or other quips to amuse future visitors.

After you finish looking, trading and signing, the next step is very important. Put everything back into the cache

---

Types of Caches

Multi-caches
This icon* indicates there is more than one cache (multiple caches) hidden on this hunt.

Some people hide a group of caches within a limited area, all tied together by clues. A hunter must use the clues from the first cache to find the second cache. Then there will be clues in the second cache to lead hunters to the third cache.

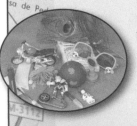

container, seal it tightly and replace it in its hiding spot exactly as it was found. That will allow someone else to enjoy the same challenges of finding the same cache.

If you find damaged items inside, make note of that so you can report it on the website after your hike. Experienced geocachers often carry a few extra plastic baggies in their packs to replace damaged or missing ones inside the caches they find.

If you are keeping track of your own finds, this is a good time to record details about the find in this book (or another notebook you're using as a personal logbook). This is especially valuable if you are searching for more than one cache on the same day; it helps you keep the information straight and accurate. It's also fun to keep track of how many finds you have made over time.

Types of Caches

There can be as many caches as the hider desires, but the hunter must find them in the correct order to be successful.

An offset cache is a variation of the multi-cache. The first set of coordinates sends hunters to someplace special, like a public statue, plaque, park bench or other fixed item. There isn't a cache hidden at that spot. Instead, there may be words or numbers on the item which are hints. The hunter then uses the clues provided on the web page to manipulate these hints to find the next cache.

continued on page 24

Geocaching Shorthand for Logbooks and/or Websites

This geocaching shorthand is especially useful in small caches when the logbook doesn't provide much writing space. Combine letters as needed to leave your message, putting a slash between each separate thought.

FTF – First to find. (I'm the first person to find this cache!)

STF – Second to find. (I'm the second person to find this cache!)

TNLN – Took nothing, left nothing. (I found the cache but I didn't take a trinket or leave a trinket; nothing was exchanged.)

T ( ), L ( ) – Took (item's name), left (item's name). (I took an item and I left an item in its place. You should include the name of each item you took and left. In a family, it is acceptable for each child to take one item but be sure to replace them with an equal number of new items.)

DNF – Did not find. (For website entry: I looked but could not find the cache.)

SL – Signed logbook. (For website entry: I signed the logbook.)

TFTC or T4TC – Thanks for the cache. (A great way to let the cache owner know you liked what s/he hid.)

TFTH or T4TH – Thanks for the hunt. (A great way to let the cache owner know you enjoyed the hike and clues.)

YAPIDKA – Yet another park I didn't know about. (A way to let the cache owner know s/he led you to a place you've never been before.)

CITO – Cache in, trash out. (I picked up trash along the way and carried it out with me.) This is also the name of a special event where geocachers join together to clean up a public area. An international CITO event is scheduled each April.

GZ – Ground Zero. This is the spot where the coordinates on your GPS receiver's screen are an exact match to the coordinates posted for a given cache. The cache may not always be located at GZ because the coordinates may be off by a small amount.

MKH – Magnetic key holder. (For website entry: This microcache is hidden in a magnetic hide-a-key box.)

NIAH – Needle in a haystack. (This small cache is hidden in an area where there are many good hiding possibilities.)

P & G or PNG – Park and grab. (For website entry: The cache is easy to find and you can get close to it with your vehicle.)

PAF – Phone a friend. (While I was geocaching, I had to call a friend on my cell phone to get more information and hints about the cache I was looking for.)

PI – Poison ivy! (I found poison ivy on my hunt. Be careful.)

R/W – Right-of-way. (The area of land between a sidewalk and street; it may be part of a clue to where a cache is hidden.)

SBA – Should be archived. (For website entry: The cache has a major problem and the owner should remove it from the website's list of active caches until it can be replaced or repaired.)

UPS or URP – Unnatural pile of sticks or unnatural rock pile. (There is a pile of sticks or rocks that doesn't look natural and points to a hidden cache.)

Report your finds online

Logged Visits (7 total.)
5 1 1

Warning. Spoilers may be included in the descriptions or links.
Cache find counts are based on the last time the page generated.

Cache Logs
May 19 by Soccer Boy Logan (47 found)
Found it with my Dad. TFTC
[view this log on a separate page]

April 22 by iamaltese (261 found)
I had some errands to do yesterday that brought me near this cache. I have metal
detected here for over 10 years; it's amazing that a whole town can disappear
almost overnight.
This is not an uncommon thing in our state. There are several hundred small towns
that did not survive here in Iowa. Pepole then thought that a town's survival meant
it needed railroad access. The whole town of Tripoli (in Bremer County) moved 1
mile south in the late 1800's just so that it would be near the "new" source of
transportation.
Thanks: for the cache!
Sorry: For the history lesson
[view this log on a separate page]

April 1 by UNIBear (617 found)
Drove out to Butler Center late this afternoon as the sun was beginning to break
through the rain clouds...it was still very windy as I drove up and down reading all

After your hunt, you may want to share your experiences with other geocachers. You can go back to the website and post an entry about each cache you found. This could include pictures you took. The key is to give kudos about the cache and also give helpful updates. But don't provide too many details because that could spoil the hunt for others. Geocachers do not like to read "spoilers" before going on an adventure.

It's especially important to report your experience if there is a problem with the cache. For example, perhaps you found the cache but it was soaking wet after the last downpour. Or you couldn't find it at all and you think it's missing. These things should be reported. Then the cache owner can check up on it and fix the problem.

Types of Caches

Tips for finding Multi-caches

Remember to allow a little more time if you are hunting for multi-caches. This is especially important if young children are part of your geocaching party. You will most likely spend more time walking, entering GPS coordinates, searching around and figuring out clues. Of course, that can offer more fun too!

continued on page 26

Website Tips

• As the sport grows, there are more websites dedicated to geocaching and a growing list of products and supplies to enhance the pastime.

In addition to general information about the sport, there are clubs, tournaments, chat forums and links to connect geocaching fans of all ages. Type in "geocaching" on a search engine and take it from there.

• A reliable and complete website to check is www.geocaching.com.

• A good site for beginners to learn about geocaching is Geocacher University (www.geocacher-u.com.)

Additional Types of Caches

Virtual Caches

Not all geocaching websites will post virtual cache locations, but this is what one icon* looks like.

In a virtual cache, there is no container to find, but there's definitely something worth finding. People who discover a beautiful view and want to share it with others might list it as a virtual cache. Maybe it's a spectacular scene at sunset, or a field of colorful spring wildflowers, or a gurgling stream surrounded by unusual rocks. Maybe it's an unusual tree formation or a special landmark. Maybe veteran geocachers would like to share a local historical marker, statue or point of interest that visitors might not otherwise know about. In these cases, they enter the coordinates for that spot and, perhaps, give hints for the best time of day or year to hunt for the cache. They do not hide an actual cache filled with trinkets, or even a log book. Their purpose is to get others to come to the site and enjoy the interesting sights they've discovered.

To prove you've found the spot, you can take a photo of yourself or your group with the "cache". In some cases, you must prove you found the correct location by posting or e-mailing an answer to a question provided by the cache owner. Then you can record your find online and in your own records, just like any other cache.

Benchmark Caches

These "treasures" are permanently-placed surveyors' markers that are part of history.

Rather than hiding an object, a geocache owner may ask people to hunt for a permanent public object used by surveyors, such as concrete posts or brass or aluminum surveyor's disks in the ground. These benchmarks also could be other manmade or natural land features that surveyors have used, such as radio towers, church spires or mountain peaks. Some of these objects might be hidden and difficult to find. Others are very obvious, and people pass by them every day without ever really seeing them.

It isn't necessary to use a GPS receiver to find most benchmarks. The clues are physical descriptions listed on the website. Benchmarks are listed by state or geographical area. They can also be found by following links from geocaching sites.

26

Additional Types of Caches

Many geocachers combine traditional cache hunting with benchmark hunts. For example, after finding an online cache listing they like, they click on a website link that says, "...all nearby benchmarks". There will be a list of benchmarks located near that cache. Once the hunter finds the cache, s/he can look for those benchmarks, too.

The fun of this type of hunt is simply in finding the marker and pondering what it indicates. How old might it be? How was it used? How many times have I walked by this area without ever noticing it? You cannot take the benchmark as they are protected by law; you simply log it as a find online and in your own record book.

Webcam Caches
This is an icon* for a webcam cache. You must stand in front of the camera to log your visit at webcam caches.

This cache uses an existing web camera that has been mounted in a public place to monitor that area, like a street intersection or park. There will not be a traditional cache to find. But to prove you have found the camera's location, you must put yourself in front of the camera and record your visit. It's helpful if a friend looks on the website that displays the photos from this camera. Then your friend can save the picture so you can officially log this cache online and in your own record book.

Not all websites post webcam locations and some technical skills are needed to save the picture and log your find correctly.

Locationless (Reverse) Caches
Instead of finding a hidden container, hunters must find a place or object according to clues given and then log its correct coordinates as shown on their GPS receiver. This is often called Waymarking and these types of "caches" can be found at the website, www.waymarking.com.

Additional Types of Caches

Cache Cams

People sometimes put an inexpensive disposable camera into their cache. When you find one, take your picture but leave the camera for the next hunter. The person who hid the cache will retrieve the camera when it's full and develop all the pictures. These pictures may be posted online for everyone to view at a later date. Don't be surprised if you see yourself! If you'd rather not be displayed online, simply sign the logbook and do not take your photo.

Puzzle Caches

These are more complicated but might be fun if you are ready for a challenge. Players must solve an online puzzle of some sort to figure out the coordinates. Only then can the players go hunting for the cache.

Mystery Caches

These caches require a player to do something else after the cache is found. The activity could be as simple as finding a code word inside the cache and reporting it to the owner, or doing something special at the site and taking a photo as proof. Only after following these instructions does a player get to record this find online.

* All cache icons shown are from the website www.geocaching.com, © of Groundspeak Inc. and are used with their permission.

What is

LETTERBOXING?

Instead of signing the logbook with your nickname (as is done in geocaching), letterboxing players "sign" with their personal rubber stamp and add some other personal notes.

Letterbox

lĕt´ər: to mark with letters; a written symbol; a printed communication sent to a recipient

bŏks: typically a rectangular container having a lid

Letterboxing is the low-tech English cousin of geocaching. No GPS receiver is required for this activity. Instead, hunters search for small waterproof containers or boxes by following cryptic clues and using their problem-solving skills while relying on a traditional compass. Successful letterboxers usually enjoy solving riddles and puzzles.

Tucked inside each letterbox is a logbook, pencil and something special: a unique rubber stamp that identifies that particular letterbox. Letterboxers also carry their own signature rubber stamp with them on their treasure hunt, as well as an ink pad and personal logbook. Upon finding a letterbox, imprints of both stamps are exchanged.

These rubber stamps usually aren't ordinary. They may be one-of-a-kind, hand-carved beauties, which is why this pastime often appeals to people with artistic flair. And just like geocaching, letterboxing is a great way to explore nature and hike some great trails through town or countryside.

The clues?
Riddles, puzzles, cryptic messages or other instructions.

The method?
To accurately decipher and follow directions and compass readings which are designed to guide you to the hidden letterbox.

The challenge?
To actually uncover the letterbox and collect some original stamp imprints.

The payoff?
The fun of the hunt and the thrill of collecting another unique inked stamp imprint in your logbook.

History of Letterboxing

People often hand out business cards (calling cards) to share information about themselves, their talents and the company where they're employed. Letterboxing began in England in the mid-1800s when a man hiked through the moors, hid his calling card in a jar and left it for others to find. According to legend, he enclosed instructions that whoever completed the hike and found his jar should add their own calling card as proof of their visit.

As this idea evolved and changed, people began hiding ("planting") boxes and enclosing self-addressed letters or postcards instead of calling cards. The instructions requested that the hiker who found the letter or postcard should take it out of the box to send it and then leave another one in its place. A new outdoor hobby was invented!

After awhile, the letters and postcards were replaced with unique rubber stamps and a logbook. Clues were shared with others, in both written form and by word of mouth, to encourage hikers to seek the letterboxes. People even published catalogs to describe the locations of the hidden letterboxes, but the catalogs were often hard to obtain.

Eventually the activity jumped across the ocean to New Hampshire when David Sobel organized a letterboxing event to promote the history and geography of the local area. It captured the imaginations of Americans, always looking for new pastimes. And with the use of computer websites to publish clues, the hobby took off in New England and beyond.

Today, there are thousands of letterboxes hidden in the United States and all over the world, and many different groups are dedicated to this new sport. In some areas, hiding the letterboxes has become a history or geography lesson for school children. Parks have organized letterboxing quests for tourists. Scout groups and other outdoor organizations are using letterboxing activities to teach orienteering skills. There are many variations for all ages and interests, so get set to go letterboxing!

Letterboxing How-Tos

5 Easy Steps

1 Gather your letterboxing supplies

- Rubber stamp
- Ink pad
- Personal logbook with unlined paper
- Pencil
- Internet access

You need a personal rubber stamp, an ink pad, a personal logbook and a pencil to carry with you on your hike. The rubber stamp can be one you purchase, one you make yourself or one you have custom-made for you. Whatever its design, the rubber stamp will be your way of signing the logbooks you find, so it should have some unique connection to your hobbies, interests or personality. It's smart to wrap it in a paper towel and keep it in a zippered plastic bag. Experienced letterboxers often carry a few heavy-duty plastic baggies and paper towels with them to repair any damaged or missing items in the letterboxes they find.

The ink pad you buy should be small enough to easily fit into your pocket but large enough to ink your rubber stamp completely. It's best if the stamping surface is raised and the ink is made with acid-free dye that dries quickly. Choose one or two fun colors of ink that will show up well on paper. You'll want to keep the pad in a sturdy zippered plastic bag.

The pages of your logbook should be unlined and large enough to hold a wide variety of stamp imprints, like those included in this book. If the book opens up flat, it is easier to make good stamp imprints. A good quality, thicker paper prevents the dye from soaking through the pages, and if the paper is also acid-free, your logbook will last longer. You should be able to tuck your logbook into your pack or pocket for easy carrying.

For letterboxing, you need clues to follow, so access to a computer and the Internet is important. The most common way to get clues is from online letterboxing websites.

Tips

Logbook – Use the special pages in this book for your first logbook entries (pages 49, 51, 53 and 100 through 121). Open the logbook on a hard, smooth surface with the pages flat. After pressing the rubber stamp on the ink pad, set the stamp down on the page without shifting it, and press down firmly to leave a clear ink imprint.

Rubber Stamps

Wrap your rubber stamp in a paper towel and pack it in a zippered baggie so the ink doesn't rub off on other objects. Directions for making your own unique rubber stamp start on page 91.

Pre-addressed

Postcards – If you find stamped and addressed postcards inside a letterbox, take one. They were enclosed by the letterbox owner. Write about your experience and mail the completed postcard back so the owner can enjoy knowing about the box s/he hid.

As with geocaching, it's important to organize your supplies before beginning your hike. You'll need a small backpack or fanny pack to hold your rubber stamp, ink pad, personal logbook, pencil, printout of the clues and other supplies. A flashlight is handy for peering into dark tree hollows or under heavy foliage. It is also smart to bring along a reliable compass, gloves and maps of the area or trail.

Since letterboxing is a hiking adventure, take along items like bandages, sunscreen, bug repellant, water and high-energy snacks. If you are letterboxing with children, bring other items as needed to make their hike enjoyable and safe. Be sure to wear comfortable shoes or hiking boots. You may want to carry along a plastic bag to pick up any trash you discover along your hike.

Types of Letterboxes

Traditional Boxes

These are similar to traditional geocache containers, but they can be smaller since they hold fewer items. Traditional letterboxes will hold a small notebook and a rubber stamp, plus perhaps a pencil and some stamped, pre-addressed postcards. Some boxes will be clear, heavy-duty plastic food containers. Others may be disguised with tape

3 Choose a letterbox to find

Go online to find one of the widely-used letterboxing websites. The websites will help you locate letterboxes hidden in your area. This is where you will find the clues too. Type in "letterboxing" or "letterboxing + clues", or go straight to the most popular site, www.letterboxing.org. This site is run by a group called Letterboxing North America and it's a good place for beginners to start.

On this site, you will find a clickable map and listing of all the states in the U.S. After clicking on a state, its map will appear and you can choose the shaded area(s) you wish to search. Then a listing of all the letterboxes in that area will be displayed. These can be sorted by their placement date (the most current placement will be listed first) or by location (with counties grouped together).

This is where the fun really begins! Each letterbox is given an interesting name. You can click on a name and read all about it. You'll find who placed the letterbox, when it was placed, what state and county it is in, the nearest city and how many boxes are hidden there.

Most important, you'll see the clues you need in order to find this letterbox. The clues are presented in many different ways.

Types of Letterboxes

or paint. Each box should be labeled well on the outside so others know it is a letterbox. The items inside usually are enclosed in zippered plastic baggies for additional protection.

Micro Boxes
Like microcaches, these letterboxes are very small. The rubber stamp inside is tiny enough to slide in and out of the container easily. Some rubber stamps fold up to fit inside. The logbook may be a

Do you like to solve riddles, figure out anagrams or use rhyming clues? Do story puzzles or imaginary historical diaries intrigue you? Do you want the challenge of using a map and compass? Maybe you'd prefer clear, straightforward instructions for your hike. Choose the type of clues you like best to help you select a letterbox to find.

Two Sample Clues

1. Go to the town located at the highest point in Houston County. Find the source of their city water to begin your hunt. (*This clue requires some research just to find your starting point.*)

2. From the home of the silver birds
   To the place that houses many words,
   Turn south and take 200 paces.
   Then step up high to watch some races.
   (*This rhyming clue provides a word puzzle to solve: Is it leading you from an airport to a bookstore to a racetrack? Or is it leading you from a high school where the Gray Hawks are the home team to the library and then to the school's stadium?*)

Types of Letterboxes

cash register tape, trimmed and rolled up inside the container. Look for plastic containers like 35mm film cans, tiny craft cases or waterproof medicine tubes used as micro boxes.

Mystery Boxes

Instead of straightforward clues with information about where to start the hunt, these clues present a story or puzzle to solve first in order to find out where to begin. There may be hidden words or a text with two different meanings. You may not even receive specific information about the state or country

Pay attention to other information offered by the letterbox owner, such as the time it takes for the hike, a description of the terrain, how difficult it may be to find the letterbox and the date the letterbox was last found or checked. If the clues use terms like "travel 10 degrees" or "head south", you will need to use a compass to help you find the letterbox. As with geocaches, treasures that have been recently found or checked are more likely to currently be in place.

When the description and clues sound just right for you, print off two copies of the information and take them along with you on your hunt. Leave one copy in your car so others will know where you are in case you get lost or need help.

Pacing Tips

Letterbox clues are often given as a number of paces. American letterboxers usually count a pace as one step. But your pace, or length of step, may be shorter or longer than the person who planted the box and wrote the clue. You can figure this out by counting your own paces between two cited landmarks and comparing that number to the number given in the clue. Then use the same ratio for other pace counts. For example, if the clue says to walk 40 paces from the fork in the path to the moss-covered bridge, and it took you 80 paces to get there, you know that you'll need to take two paces for every one pace listed in the clues.

Types of Letterboxes

the letterbox is hidden in! Although these letterboxes may be too challenging for beginners, they can be very exciting for experienced letterboxers.

Bonus Boxes and Add-ons

The clues to finding a bonus box are not posted on a website. Instead, they are hidden inside another letterbox called a host. After finding the host box, a letterboxer can follow these clues to

Start your hunt!

Read through all the clues, from start to finish, before taking off on your adventure. The clues may tell you to count things along the way or to look for specific markers. Always note where you've parked your car too, as the clues will not tell you how to get back. You may consider taking a GPS receiver along, not for finding the letterbox, but to mark the car as a waypoint.

Then head out, following the directions carefully, one clue at a time. Use a compass if clues use the terms "degrees" or "bearing" and look for any landmarks cited in the instructions. As you arrive at each landmark, make notes about the location. What does it look like? Which direction is it from the trail? What other things are nearby? This will help if you must backtrack. It may also help you find your way back to the starting point if you become turned around.

Remember that when clues specify a number of paces to take, you may need to count and calibrate your own pacing to

Types of Letterboxes

find the bonus box, which is usually hidden somewhere nearby. The clues remain inside the host box for others to discover the surprise letterboxing challenge.

If a new hunt uses an existing letterbox location as the starting point for the hunt, it is called an add-on. Clues are posted online so people know there will be two boxes to find, but they must find the first letterbox before they are able to follow the clues to the add-on box.

continued on page 43

match the planter's pace. Refer to page 37 for specific details on this topic.

Some clues tell you the number of minutes you must walk to reach a certain landmark or the letterbox itself. But your speed of walking may be different than the clue writer's so you may not be able to rely on those clues alone. By combining the time clues with landmark or pacing clues and comparing the minutes you've actually walked as you arrive at points along the way, you will gain valuable information and a way of double-checking your route.

Which way to go?
Simple Reminders about Directions

Many letterbox clues will require a basic knowledge of north, south, east and west directions. An easy way to remember their order is by noting the location of the sun. The sun rises in the east and sets in the west. At noon, the sun is high in the sky but slightly to the south (unless you live in the southern hemisphere). If you are walking north around lunchtime, the sun should be behind you.

Another way to remember the order and relationship of directions is to memorize a phrase like the traditional "Never Eat Shredded Wheat", or an updated one, "Now Every Seeker Wins". The directions move clockwise around the compass, starting at 12 o'clock. If you are walking north and your clue tells you to turn east, you should turn to your right.

Right hand or left hand? Help children with this easy-to-remember clue. With tops of hands in front of you, make an L shape with the thumb and pointer finger of both hands. Whichever hand makes the L in the correct direction for you is your left hand.

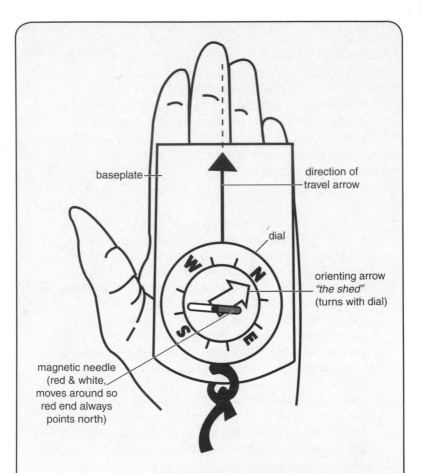

baseplate

direction of travel arrow

dial

orienting arrow *"the shed"* (turns with dial)

magnetic needle (red & white, moves around so red end always points north)

Tips for using a compass

You will need a compass if the letterbox clues use the words degrees, bearing, heading or azimuth.

To use the compass correctly with degree clues provided in a letterbox:

1. Find the dial on the compass. Turn it so the number of degrees listed in the clue matches up with the line on the baseplate, called the "direction-of-travel arrow". You have just dialed in the bearing. (Bearing is the direction you should travel to stay on course or head toward an object, measured in degrees on a compass. Bearing can also be called heading or azimuth.)

2. Hold the compass in front of you in your hand, flat and steady, with the direction-of-travel arrow pointing forward. Slowly turn your body until the red moving arrow (the magnetic needle) lines up with the red arrow outline below it (the orienting arrow). A common phrase used to remember this step is "put red in the shed".

3. Now look at the direction-of-travel arrow on the baseplate. This is the direction you need to walk. But, before you take off, look far ahead in the direction the arrow points. Do you see any distinct landmarks, trees or rocks straight ahead? If so, head toward those landmarks as you begin your hunt. Then you won't have to stare down at the compass as you walk and you'll be able to pay attention to other things around you. When you reach the first landmark, check to be sure "red is still in the shed" and you are still walking in the direction that the direction-of-travel arrow is pointing. Find another landmark in the right direction and continue to walk. (If you can't find a landmark, ask a friend to act as a landmark by walking a distance ahead of you in the correct direction and then stopping. You can walk until you catch up to the friend and then repeat the process, using the compass to point your friend in the right direction.)

4. To find your way back, reverse the bearing by 180° in the opposite direction. (A simple method is to turn the compass until the white part of the arrow is in the open red arrow outline below it, or "put white in the shed".)

To find the bearing of a landmark or letterbox for which you want to write clues:
Try "shooting a bearing" at items around home before you go hiking. For example, find a flagpole or other item in the distance. Hold the compass in front of you and turn your body until the direction-of-travel arrow points toward the pole. Then turn the dial on the compass until the red moving arrow (magnetic needle) is lined up with the red arrow on the baseplate ("put red in the shed"). Look at the degree number on the dial that lines up with the direction-of-travel arrow. That is your bearing for this flagpole. Follow this process to find the bearing for a landmark or letterbox.

True North

The magnetic arrow (the freely-moving red arrow) always points to the magnetic north. Bearings in clues can be based on magnetic north or true north. Most letterboxes give clues with magnetic bearings so you can use your compass just as it reads. If the clues are based on true north however, you will need to factor in the magnetic declination that affects the area of the country where you are located. It becomes a simple task to add or subtract the correct number of degrees of declination and set your compass accordingly. Go online to the National Geophysical Data Center website at www.ngdc.noaa.gov and use the information to help you adjust your compass correctly.

Tip: *When holding the compass while walking, it can be helpful to place it in the palm of your hand with your middle finger lined up with the direction-of-travel arrow.*

You've followed the clues and think you've arrived at the exact spot of the letterbox, but you don't see it. Now what should you do? Search around for it! Be careful not to dig things up or pull things apart.  The letterbox won't be hidden that way. Reread your clues to see what you've missed. Don't forget to look up and down, as well as at eye level. You may need to kneel down or stoop over to look into objects like hollow logs or a rock's crevice.

Once you've found the letterbox, it's time to enjoy the contents of the treasure. But since letterboxing is secretive by nature, take the box away from its hiding spot and do your perusing where others will not see you. Find a quiet place to sit down and open the box. Read the logbook messages to find out about the other people who have successfully found that same box. Look closely at the stamp imprints on the pages. Do you recognize any of them from other letterbox finds?

Types of Letterboxes

Themed Boxes

Some letterboxes are hidden for only a short time for special holidays or events. For example, the clues, rubber stamp and hiding spot might relate to Christmas and may only be hidden and found throughout the month of December.

Then it's time to "stamp in". Using your personal rubber stamp, make an imprint in the letterbox logbook and write a short message for others to enjoy. Be sure to keep your comments positive.

The final fun comes with collecting a new stamp imprint in your own logbook. Remove the rubber stamp from the letterbox and ink it on your ink pad. Then make a print on the logbook pages included in this book or another logbook. (It may be a good idea to try out the stamp on your clue sheet before stamping your logbook, just to be sure the stamp works well.)

When you've finished enjoying the letterbox, repack everything and tuck the container back into its original hiding spot exactly as it was found. Do not leave it unhidden. If the zippered plastic baggies or paper towels are damaged or missing, you may replace them with new ones, if you carry any of these supplies in your gear.

Types of Letterboxes

Others

Letterboxing is a perfect companion to some other hobbies. For example, letterbox clues can lead history buffs to ghost towns, aircraft crash sites or other places of little-known historical importance. Through historical narratives and trivia, hobbyists can enjoy using letterboxing clues to solve puzzles and find the correct locations, even if they aren't interested in collecting stamp imprints.

Stamp Designs

You will often find that the rubber stamp inside each letterbox has a shape or design that is linked to the location where it is hidden. It may even have an imprint of the name of the area, which makes each hunt unique and memorable. As you collect and recall your finds, you'll collect a visual travel log of the areas you've visited. For example, if you are hunting in the foothills of an Arizona mountain range, the stamp may be a picture of a winding mountain trail with a cactus. (Even the style of logbook or postcards in the letterbox may tie into the same theme.)

Lettercaches? Geoboxes?

What's that all about? Some people are blending geocaching with letterboxing. These hybrids contain a rubber stamp and logbook like letterboxing, plus clues that require the use of a GPS receiver, like geocaching. There may be other clues and riddles provided for the hunt, as in a traditional letterbox, and trinkets may be added for trading, as in a traditional geocache.

When they find the treasure, letterboxers can exchange stamps, geocachers can select or trade prizes and both can chalk it up as one more find.

The Language of Letterboxing

Signature stamp – The rubber stamp found inside a letterbox becomes the signature stamp of that box. It also refers to the personal stamp a letterboxer carries and uses consistently to stamp in letterbox logbooks in order to leave a "signature".

Stamping in – After finding a letterbox, players use their personal rubber stamp to make a print in the letterbox's logbook. Then they use the stamp found inside the letterbox to make a print in their own logbook.

Trail name – A letterboxer's nickname, which may be used when stamping in and writing entries on websites.

Planted – Another word for placed. The person who assembles, owns and hides a letterbox "plants" the box for others to find.

Hitchhiker – Like the travel bug or hitchhiker from geocaching, this is a traveling letterbox found inside another letterbox. It could be just a rubber stamp and logbook. The finder is supposed to remove the traveling portion and take it to another box.

Traveler (or Personal traveler) – This is a special rubber stamp that a letterboxer carries for one purpose: to keep his or her signature stamp a secret in case another letterboxer is met along the way. When meeting a fellow hunter, the two can exchange images of their traveler stamps, without revealing their signature stamps.

PF count – The number of boxes hidden or placed (P) and the number of boxes found (F). Some letterboxers keep records of these things and may add this information in their e-mail messages or when they sign logbooks. A box can be counted only once.

X or E count – The number of stamps personally exchanged with other letterboxers (X) and the number of stamps collected at a letterboxing event (E), such as a gathering. Some people include this information in e-mail messages or logbooks.

FF – The first person to find a letterbox (First Find). Some letterboxers keep track of their FFs and sometimes FF certificates are included in newly planted letterboxes as a reward to the person who finds it first.

WoM clues – Clues that are not posted on websites for general use, but rather are passed by word of mouth (from person to person). They may be written down, but only if they are concealed or encrypted in some way.

Bearing – On a compass, a direction measured in degrees, usually from magnetic north. This direction is needed to stay on course as you head toward a destination. (Other names for this are azimuth and heading.) For example, part of a clue could read, "A sharp twist to the south means you're almost on top. 212 degrees takes you to this letterbox" means you'll need to move toward the 212 degree mark on your compass after you turn to the south.

Cuckoo clues – Clues that are not posted online, but are left in letterboxes and travel, like hitchhikers, between boxes. A person who finds a cuckoo clue can copy it and keep it for later use. Then s/he may take it and hide it in a different letterbox for another hunter to find.

Box in, bag out – The practice of bringing a plastic trash bag while letterboxing in order to pick up trash along the way and carry it out to be discarded. This is like geocaching's CITO.

BYOI – Bring your own ink. Some online postings give this note so you'll know that no ink pad is included in the letterbox. As a general rule, however, it's always wise to carry your own ink pad since many boxes do not provide one or may contain an ink pad that no longer works.

Letterboxing Logbook

Directions

The next few pages can be used as your personal logbook.
Record the date and location of each find, then make a clear
impression of the stamp and jot down a few notes about
your find.

To make clean, clear impressions, open this book on a flat,
even surface. Press the rubber stamp on a premium dye ink
pad. Check to make sure you have inked the entire stamp
surface. Then firmly press the stamp on the page. It's a good
idea to practice making imprints on scratch paper before
making prints in this logbook. When you are satisfied with
your technique, start filling up these pages!

Date_____

Location_____

Date_____

Location_____

Date_____

Location_____

Date_____

Location_____

Date_____

Location_____

Date_____

Location_____

Date_____

Location_____

Date_____

Location_____

Date_____

Location_____

PACK IT, HIDE IT, POST IT!

It's just as much fun to pack and hide a geocache or letterbox as it is to hunt for one. After you have successfully uncovered a few hidden treasures, you will know what makes a good one – and you might be ready to hide one of your own!

Pack It

Whether packing a geocache or letterbox, it's important to plan what you'll put inside. All the items should be placed in heavy-duty zippered plastic baggies. Close the bags tightly before placing them into your container so all items are protected from damage. Here are some more guidelines...

What to put inside

- **Logbook and pencil** – A logbook should be included in every geocache or letterbox, and if the container is large enough, a sharpened pencil or working pen should also be inside. (Letterboxers prefer thick pages of unruled paper, at least 2 inches square.) It's smart to place these things in their own sealed plastic bag.

- **Letter** – Enclose a letter which explains that this container is part of a world-wide treasure hunting game called geocaching (or letterboxing) and list some of the basic rules. It's a great way to introduce the public to this sport and politely ask them to leave the treasure as they found it. Websites offer some letter examples or you can use the samples on page 59.

- **For Letterboxes – a rubber stamp** – Wrap the stamp in a paper towel and place it in a zippered plastic bag. It's nice if the provided stamp has a design that relates to that particular letterbox and its location, such as an owl stamp for a wooded area inhabited by bard owls.

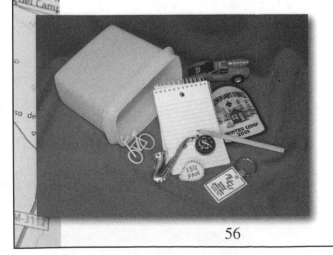

Optional items to put inside

- **Optional for Geocaches – trinkets –** Include some small items that can be examined or traded. These are most interesting if they represent a local angle of some sort. For example, a recipe with local ethnic appeal or a keychain imprinted with the name and picture of a nearby lake would be fun for geocachers to collect. An average cost is $1 to $3 per item.

- **Optional for Geocaches – disposable camera –** A camera can be included so visitors to the cache can take their own photo. Also, you may want to include a note to ask visitors to write down the number of the photo next to their logbook entry so they can report it online and you can match up each picture with the correct geocacher.

- **Optional for Letterboxes – stamped, self-addressed postcards –** These can be included so people who find your letterbox can write on the postcard and send it back to you. It's a fun way for you to see what's happening with the letterbox you planted.

- **Optional for Geocaches and Letterboxes – hitchhikers or travel bugs –** These items can be tucked inside with a note of instruction. The note can be as simple as "Take me all over the world," or it may list someplace more specific like "Take me to Colorado." For geocaches, it's a small trinket with or without a special travel bug tag. For letterboxes, hitchhikers consist of an extra rubber stamp that is meant to be taken and then moved to another letterbox location.

What NOT to put inside

- **No food**. Animals will go after food and ruin the hidden treasure. In fact, before handling the treasure, it's important to wash your hands well so your scent won't transfer.
- **No weapons, lighters or fireworks**. Children could find these dangerous items and harm themselves.
- **No alcohol, tobacco products, drugs or drug-related supplies.** Every object should be legal and safe for all ages.
- **No pornography or morally questionable items**. This is a family-friendly sport so use common sense.

Letters

It's important to clearly label your geocache or letterbox so the public knows what the item is, whether they are intentionally looking for it or not. Use the samples on the next page to create your personal messages. Attach the message to the side or lid of the container or tuck one inside before hiding the box. Type or print the letter on sturdy paper and cover it with clear contact paper, packing tape or lamination plastic so it is waterproof. If you wish to include a longer letter with more information, simply place the paper inside a sealed plastic bag and tuck it inside the cache or letterbox with the other items.

Sample Letters

Be creative and personalize them with
colorful or camouflaged paper, stickers or designs.

Geocache letter sample:

Geocache Site: Please read this!

This box is part of a worldwide GPS scavenger hunt called geocaching. If you found the container accidentally and are not interested in playing the game, please do not disturb the box, its contents or its hiding place.

Players use GPS receivers to hide and hunt for treasures like this. The coordinates for each hiding spot are listed on the Internet. The rules are simple: If you take a trinket from the cache, you must leave something of similar or greater value in its place. (Please do not take the camera; you may take your photo however.) Write about your experience in the logbook, sign and date it.

To find coordinates for other caches or to learn more about geocaching, visit www.geocaching.com. Thank you.

Name of Cache: _____

Placed: _____ *(date)* Coordinates:_____

Letterbox sample:

You have found a letterbox! Congratulations!

This box was packed and hidden as part of a national treasure-hunting game called letterboxing. If you are interested in playing this game, please find the rubber stamp inside, make an imprint on paper, then read and sign the logbook. Replace the items and hide the box exactly as you found it for the next person to find.

If you do not wish to play, please do not disturb this container or its contents. To learn more about this game, visit www.letterboxing.org online. Thank you.

Name of Letterbox: _____

Placed: _____ *(date)*

Leaving a "Signature" Item

When geocachers become skilled pros at this sport, some like to put a special "signature" item into every cache they hide. Like a business card, this item is personal and tells something about the individual who placed the cache. For a woodcarving hobbyist, it could be something unique like a hand-carved wood figure. For an electrician, it could be a mini-flashlight with a company's logo. For a family, it could be a wooden nickel or flat rock with an imprint of their family crest. It could even be a simple phrase or sketch that is repeated in every logbook. Then each time someone finds that special signature item or reads that familiar entry, they'll know which geocacher hid the cache.

The Right Container

Choose a container that is large enough to hold your items but small enough to be hidden well. It's very important that the container itself is weatherproof and durable, even though the items inside may also be packed inside a sealed plastic bag. If the trinkets and logbook inside your cache become wet from rain or snow, they may be ruined. At the very least, they become soggy, smelly and unpleasant to find.

The cache or letterbox container also must be resealable, because after people find it, they should be able to close it securely for the next person. Plastic resealable food storage containers work well if they are heavy-duty and made for freezer use. Clear containers have the benefit of being see-through so hunters know what they are finding right away.

The containers must hold up well in both freezing and hot temperatures. Although it may be tempting to use cheap disposable plastic containers such as those from a deli or packaged food, generally these do not hold up well for caches because they tend to crack. A better choice would be sturdy plastic containers designed for freezer use.

Nalgene water bottles work well in all kinds of weather, but never use glass or other breakable materials. Avoid containers that originally held food too, such as peanut butter jars. These could attract animals.

Army surplus ammo cans and 5-gallon buckets are favorites among geocachers needing large containers. Plastic film cans are popular for micro containers

Label the outside of any container with a permanent waterproof marker or paint pen with a title like "Official Geocache" or "This is a Letterbox". Then authorities won't think it's an abandoned, illegal or dangerous package. It also helps people who discover the container by accident know what they've found. Hopefully they'll be respectful and replace it as they found it, or they will read your letter of explanation and become interested in a new hobby!

Disguised Containers

Some owners disguise the containers. They creatively use camouflage duct tape or paints to make the cache or letterbox more difficult to find. In some cases, they

camouflage the container for safety reasons. For example, military containers are wonderful for caches but they should be painted or covered to hide the military label and then labeled clearly as a geocache.

Checklist

When choosing a container, ask yourself these questions:

❑ Will it keep water out?

❑ Will it hold up in heat, humidity, snow and freezing temperatures?

❑ Will it be easy enough for others to open and reseal?

❑ Is it unbreakable?

❑ Will it be recognizable as a cache or letterbox and not mistaken for something dangerous?

Examples of good containers
(new or never used to hold food)

Examples of poor containers
(too brittle or flimsy, breakable, used to hold food)

Hide It

It's important to choose a good spot to hide the cache or letterbox. Here are some things to consider...

Choose an area that is interesting and legal

A large part of the fun of geocaching and letterboxing is hiking to new areas and discovering something interesting or beautiful. Therefore, when deciding on a hiding spot for your treasure, be creative! Try to share places that might otherwise be bypassed. As you hike, pay attention to special land or vegetation features.

If you take the easy way out and just hide the container behind an ordinary rock along an ordinary trail with ordinary scenery, it will be an ordinary hunt. But if the rock is shaped like familiar mouse ears and the trail has beautiful wildflowers with a river view and bald eagles soaring above, it will be an extraordinary and memorable one.

If you are not hiding the cache or letterbox on your own land, you must get permission to hide it from the landowner or the property manager. Many geocachers will visit this spot after it is posted on a website, so it must be placed in an area that won't be damaged by foot traffic. If the location invades the privacy of the property owners, they may not agree to be a host for the cache.

Areas operated by the National Park Service or U.S. Fish and Wildlife Service (like wildlife refuges) do not permit geocaching. Caches must not be hidden near military installations or public structures either, since bridges, dams, government buildings, airports and schools are considered possible targets for terrorist attacks. It is unwise to hide caches or letterboxes near heavy traffic or other places that could be dangerous to hunters or suspicious to law enforcement personnel.

Cemeteries or burial grounds are also off-limits. A good rule of thumb is to avoid any recreational activities in areas that are sacred or spiritual places to a group of people.

However, local, county and state parks can be great places to hide caches. It's wise to ask permission from the park rangers to find out the current rules. It is possible that certain areas are off-limits. The general rule for geocaching is to leave nature as undisturbed as possible.

Playing the game indoors

A cache or letterbox doesn't have to be outdoors. Some interesting urban treasures can be hidden inside buildings, such as libraries. Of course, this should only be done with permission from the person in charge.

Choose an area that is safe and accessible

Part of the game of geocaching or letterboxing is to disguise the hidden cache or letterbox. But it's very important that all treasures are safely hidden and accessible to hunters. Even if a branch sticking out from a 40-foot cliff would be a great hiding spot, it's not a good idea. People should not have to risk their lives to reach a geocache or letterbox. Always use common sense and choose places that can be reached safely.

Another thing to consider when hiding a container is the change in seasons. Is this treasure hidden in an area with four different seasons? If summertime foliage disguises a treasure well, how will it look in the winter when all the leaves are gone? These changes might force you to alter clues as well. How might changing weather conditions affect safety? If the trek could become dangerous in muddy conditions, rethink your plan.

If you think your treasure will attract quite a few people, hide it where constant foot traffic won't give it away. If people beat down a path through the grass to find it, this "social trail" will give away the hiding spot so it won't be much of a mystery to future hunters. It's also nice if hunters can take the cache or letterbox to a nearby private area, away from the hiding spot, to examine the contents. This calls less attention to the cache or letterbox and doesn't ruin it for other potential hunters.

One last word on safety: Be aware of the surroundings. If you found a great hiding spot but it's in the middle of a patch of poison ivy or next to a busy street, near railroad tracks or in a high crime area, you should find another spot.

Special Tips for Hiding Letterboxes
If you find a special place you'd like to hide the letterbox, make sure that place lends itself to clear clues and landmarks that will be easy to identify. Spend time looking around the area to pick out landmarks or other unique features nearby that can be used for clues. Take note of these and then work backward from the hiding place to the start of the hunt as you jot down information. This will help you write your clues.

How to hide the cache or box

- Look for openings that could be hiding spots. Slide your treasure into a rotten log or knot hole in a tree. In urban areas, check concrete parking blocks.

- Cover it. Scatter dry grass or pine needles on top of it. Letterboxers call this process of disguising the location with leaves or forest debris "blessing" it.

- Set it under something. Put it underneath something that can act as an anchor, like a unique rock or a ledge.

- Choose a spot that has many other potential hiding spots around it so hunters will need to search carefully to find it.

How NOT to hide the cache or box

- In plain sight. If you leave it lying out in the open, there is no challenge for hunters. It may be too obvious and too easy for muggles (non-geocachers) to stumble upon it accidentally.

- Too well-hidden. Don't hide it so well that people are not able to find it in a reasonable amount of time.

- Buried. Caches or boxes should never be buried underground. Not only does that disturb and deface the area, but geocachers and letterboxers aren't prepared to dig.

Geocaches
How to record the location of the cache with accurate latitude and longitude coordinates

When you have hidden your cache, you'll need to figure out the correct location of the hiding spot on your GPSr. Although latitude and longitude readings may not be 100 percent perfect, you need to get them as accurate as possible. Be sure your GPS receiver is getting a good signal before recording the coordinates. Follow the instructions on your GPS receiver to enter the coordinates correctly.

After recording one set, walk away, come back and check the numbers several more times. This ensures your figures are as accurate as possible. You may need to use an average of the numbers you recorded. You can print the coordinates on the outside of your container and inside your logbook too. This helps finders double-check their data.

Record other hints you'll want to include on the website posting, such as an encrypted clue that would help people find the cache. Try to accurately judge how difficult this cache will be to find. Judge the terrain as well. Is it a flat, easy, short hike or one that requires great energy, patience and fitness? Jot all these things down on paper so you won't forget the details.

Letterboxes
How to invent fun clues and record distances between them

When you have hidden your letterbox near or under an easy-to-identify feature, look back at your list of possible landmarks. Then walk back on the path, counting your paces and figuring out the directions, turns and location of landmarks. It's good to include some landmarks scattered along the way so the hunters can check their progress and know they are going in the right direction toward the letterbox. This is also a good way for hunters to calibrate their paces. It is especially fun for children to look for the landmarks or other special features mentioned in the clues.

The mention of landmarks doesn't have to be boring or straightforward! You might say, "A sleeping giant named Rocky is yawning on your left" to indicate the mouth of a large cave that is to the hunter's left. Until the letterboxers reach that spot, they may not know what the clue is indicating. But, upon seeing the cave, they will be reassured they are definitely on the right path.

If you want groups of people to search for a letterbox over an extended period of time, it's best not to use landmarks that could change or disappear over time. For example, rotting trees can fall over and be cleared away, but boulders and fences are more permanent.

Sometimes letterboxers include clues that are "catching" features. These are intended to catch the hunters and stop them before they go too far in the wrong direction. An example of a catch feature is, "If you reach the barbed wire fence, you've gone too far." These are handy if the other clues are tricky.

"Go 50 paces until you reach a Y in the path." This type of clue can be helpful near the beginning of your directions. By pairing a pace clue with a specific destination, like a Y in the path, hunters can figure out how their pace compares to yours. Since each person's pace is a little different, letterboxers should count their steps to the Y in the path and compare it to 50. Then they can use that same formula each time the riddle mentions paces. The word "step" can also be substituted for the word "pace".

After you have all your landmarks, paces and clues jotted down, it's time to combine them into fun riddles, rhymes, stories, puzzles, maps or other clues to share online. Use your imagination and write something fun for letterboxers to read and follow!

How to be a responsible owner of your hidden cache or letterbox

Hiding a cache or planting a letterbox is almost like getting a pet; it is very important to take care of it from that point on! Hide your cache or letterbox in an area that you can watch over, visit and check regularly. It should be close enough to home that you will be able to maintain it well. You can also check its status on the website often to read what others are saying. If it is damaged or lost, it is your responsibility to fix, remove or replace the cache or letterbox.

If you must remove it, go back to the website and delete the listing for that cache or letterbox. Otherwise people will go hunting for it and become frustrated when it cannot be found.

Out-of-the-Ordinary Hiding Ideas and Finds

Log Cache – On property you own, cut a fallen log in half, hollow out the center of both pieces and tuck the cache inside the hollow. Then put the log pieces back together again and place the log in a natural setting. Hints could include the size of the log, other objects that surround it or on which side of the trail it is hidden.

Campus Cache – Caches have been hidden around college campuses to encourage alumni and students to discover hidden attractions off the beaten path, such as an unusual sculpture.

Birdhouse Cache – An abandoned birdhouse makes a fun hiding spot for a micro.

Creeping Cache – Attach a big plastic spider or other creeping critter to a micro as a disguise to give hunters a little shiver of fright and delight. If you're clever, rig it to move along a string when a nearby stick is moved.

Kitten Cache – While geocaching in a county park, in addition to discovering the planned cache, one family also found an abandoned mother cat and her seven small babies – a lucky catch for both families!

Post It

Posting a hidden treasure

For others to find the cache or box you have hidden, it must be posted and described accurately on a reliable website. Here are some things to remember...

Geocache Postings

Choose a geocaching website to advertise your hide. For successful hunting, include enough information about the cache so people are curious and will want to hunt for it. You should include these things:

1. **Cache name** – Give the cache a **name** that is fun or interesting. The name can offer hints about what type of cache it is or where it is hidden, such as "Minnie Wood" (a micro or small traditional cache that's hidden in or around trees).

2. **Type** – Describe what **type of cache** it is, such as a traditional, micro, virtual or letterbox hybrid.

3. **Size** – List the size of traditional caches so people have a better idea of what they are searching for. Labeling a cache as small, medium or large is generally adequate information.

4. **Who hid it?** – Include your geocaching nickname. If people like the way you make and hide your caches, they'll search for listings of other ones you've hidden.

5. **Coordinates** – List the accurate latitude and longitude coordinates.

6. **World location** – Record the state and country where the cache is hidden. (Hunters will be able to search by ZIP code or nearest city.)

7. **Date** – Record the date you hid the cache. If it is a very recent hide, seekers may try to be the first person to find it ("FTF"). Most likely, recent hides are still in place, making them good choices for beginners.

8. Difficulty and Terrain Ratings – Evaluate two different things – how hard it will be to find the cache and what sort of terrain will be crossed in order to find the cache. (Each part can be rated on a scale, generally 1 to 5 stars, and the website will help you rate your cache correctly. It's important to be as accurate as possible so people can choose the hike that's right for them.)

Easy, Average, Challenging, Difficult or Extreme?

For family geocaching, look at the following things carefully when choosing a cache to try to find.

How difficult will it be to find the cache?

Caches that are hidden in relatively plain view and can be found quickly are the easiest (★). Others may require more poking around and could take 30 minutes or more to find after you've hiked to/reached the right area (★★). The most difficult ones could take multiple days and require the use of special sports equipment (★★★★★).

How difficult will the hike be?

Terrain that earns the easiest rating is probably paved, flat and less than ½ mile long. A stroller or wheelchair can be used in this type of hunt (★). An average terrain is still good for children because the walking is relatively easy and unobstructed, and it is usually shorter than 2 miles (★★).

As difficulty increases, the hiker must hike further distances off-trail, through overgrowth, and perhaps do some climbing. Therefore, the number of stars posted on the website increases (up to ★★★★★).

9. Comments – You may want to add a few comments to briefly explain what makes this cache special without giving away its location. You can also describe what the cache container looks like. For example, maybe this is a cache that is best found on a night hike. If it's particularly good for young families, it might be worth mentioning. You can also post attributes using icons on some websites. These give additional tips about things like hazards nearby, whether parking is available or if there is a scenic view.

10. Coded clues and key – Add a short clue, but put it in a simple encrypted code so hunters can choose whether or not to decipher the clue. The most common geocaching code, shown below, is a simple alphabet code called "Rot13" or "Rotate 13". Each letter in the code equals the letter above or below it.

A	B	C	D	E	F	G	H	I	J	K	L	M
N	O	P	Q	R	S	T	U	V	W	X	Y	Z

Example

Encrypted Clue   RNFG BS SYNTCBYR

Decoded Solution EAST OF FLAGPOLE

11. Optional photos – It is possible to upload photos of the area where the cache is hidden. If people see a beautiful stream or wooded walking trail, they may decide this is the cache for which to search. Be careful not to spoil the hunt by showing too many details though.

Tips

On your postings, give as much additional information as you can that could help families choose appropriate hikes. If your cache is along a flat, paved route, then a family with a child in a stroller or on a bicycle could hunt for this one. If it's particularly family-friendly because of a playground or recreational activity nearby, that's a good thing to note. Families may also like to know if there is a restroom and picnic table available.

On the other hand, if the area is very rocky, sandy or the climbing is steep, it's helpful to know that as well. Even if that cache is nearby, a family with small children may feel that type is too difficult and may want to choose a different one.

Some websites' icons show these types of atributes at a glance. That makes it very easy to pick and choose hikes which are right for a particular group.

A Typical Geocache Posting

This is the type of information you will see on a typical geocaching website page. It describes a particular cache. Hunters can read about it and decide if this is a cache they want to seek.

It includes a coded clue to be decrypted. (You can also read some of the comments geocachers have posted after they've found this cache.) This posting is from the website www. geocaching.com.

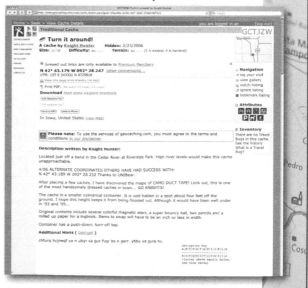

Geo-Storming!

Do a little brainstorming and jot down your great ideas for geocache names, trinkets you might collect and places to hide them. Consider themes you might follow for various caches.

Fun cache names or themes: _____

_____

_____

_____

_____

Trinkets to collect and include: _____

_____

_____

_____

_____

Places to hide them:_____

_____

_____

_____

_____

Other ideas: _____

_____

_____

_____

_____

Letterbox Postings

Choose a letterboxing website and advertise your hide. The information you provide is similar to cache details. For successful hunting, include enough information about the letterbox so people are curious and will want to hunt for it. Record these things:

1. **Letterbox name** – Pick a fun, unusual or clue-filled name for the letterbox.

2. **Who hid it?** – This is your letterboxing nickname so others will know who owns and hid this box.

3. **Placement date** – Record the date you planted the box. Again, recent hides are most likely still in place, which is good for beginners.

4. **State, county and nearest city** – This helps hunters choose a letterbox within the area they want to hunt.

5. **Number of boxes** – You may hide one or more letterboxes using the same clue. Let hunters know how many boxes they will be looking for.

6. **Clues** – These should include a riddle, story, puzzle or other format for clues that can be followed to lead the hunter(s) to the letterbox. They can be written creatively or straightforward but must be accurate. Quite often there is basic information about the park or area, including historical or cultural tidbits. Your clues may offer other helpful information, including:
   - a difficulty rating (for example, Easy or Suitable for Families)
   - terrain description
   - length of hike or time that should be allowed to complete the hike
   - if a compass is recommended
   - type of letterbox hidden (size, appearance or other details)
   - the date it was last checked or maintained (You should update your listing periodically to insure data is current.)

7. Additional information – It is helpful to give people more information if it applies to your letterbox such as:

- if the area is highly traveled and secrecy is needed while hunting
- if dogs are allowed in the area
- if there is an entrance fee for the hiking area
- if there are particular hazards or poisonous plants nearby
- if the box is hidden in a wheelchair-accessible area

A Typical Letterbox Posting

This is the type of information you will see on a letterboxing website page. It describes a particular letterbox and its location. Letterboxers can read the clues and location and decide if this is a letterbox they want to seek. There are directions, clues and sometimes, special notices, to help the letterboxer be successful.

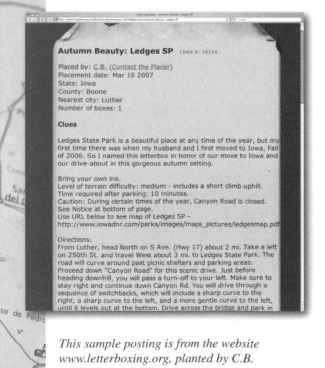

Autumn Beauty: Ledges SP   LDNA #: 29216

Placed by: C.B. (Contact the Placer)
Placement date: Mar 16 2007
State: Iowa
County: Boone
Nearest city: Luther
Number of boxes: 1

Clues

Ledges State Park is a beautiful place at any time of the year, but my first time there was when my husband and I first moved to Iowa, Fall of 2006. So I named this letterbox in honor of our move to Iowa and our drive-about in this gorgeous autumn setting.

Bring your own ink.
Level of terrain difficulty: medium - includes a short climb uphill.
Time required after parking: 10 minutes.
Caution: During certain times of the year, Canyon Road is closed.
See Notice at bottom of page.
Use URL below to see map of Ledges SP -
http://www.iowadnr.com/parks/images/maps_pictures/ledgesmap.pdf

Directions:
From Luther, head North on S Ave. (Hwy 17) about 2 mi. Take a left on 250th St. and travel West about 3 mi. to Ledges State Park. The road will curve around past picnic shelters and parking areas. Proceed down "Canyon Road" for this scenic drive. Just before heading downhill, you will pass a turn-off to your left. Make sure to stay right and continue down Canyon Rd. You will drive through a sequence of switchbacks, which will include a sharp curve to the right, a sharp curve to the left, and a more gentle curve to the left, until it levels out at the bottom. Drive across the bridge and park in

This sample posting is from the website
www.letterboxing.org, planted by C.B.

The
SAFE & COURTEOUS
Treasure Hunter

Safety while Hiking

- Get a hiking partner. It's not safe to go into the woods or remote spots alone.

- Tell someone where you are going and when you will return. Leave a copy of the cache or letterbox information in your car. That way, if you should become lost, people will know where to look for you.

- Take along a compass and know how to use it properly. In case your GPS receiver loses power or can't get an accurate reading, the compass can help you figure out your location.

- Take water to drink.

- Check the weather forecast before starting your hunt. Then watch the skies and pay attention to time as you hunt. It's not fun if you have to turn around in the dark before reaching your goal or seek shelter in a raging thunderstorm.

- Wear the right clothing for the weather and landscape. If you have to crawl through underbrush where ticks and thorns reside, it is smart to wear long pants and a shirt with long sleeves. Comfortable shoes or boots will make the hike much more enjoyable. A hat and sunglasses will protect you from the sun's burning rays on a clear day, and a rain poncho is good to have when the weather is unpredictable.

- If it is game-hunting season in a particular area, choose a different day or area for your treasure hunt. Wear blaze orange vests and clothing as needed.

- Do not touch discarded materials that could be hazardous, such as broken glass, chemical or medical containers, coffee filters, or gas cans.

- Look up from your GPS receiver or compass regularly and pay attention to things around you to avoid holes, branches or other dangers.

- Watch out for poisonous plants and critters, including poison ivy, poison oak or snakes sunning themselves on a warm rock or trail.

Poison Ivy? Poison Oak? Poison Sumac?

"Leaves of three, let it be." This statement can help you identify poison ivy and poison oak. Contact with these plants or poison sumac may cause reactions and skin problems for some people. These irritating leaves may also appear in groups of five to nine. In addition, if you see small yellow or white berries on these plants, stay away from them.

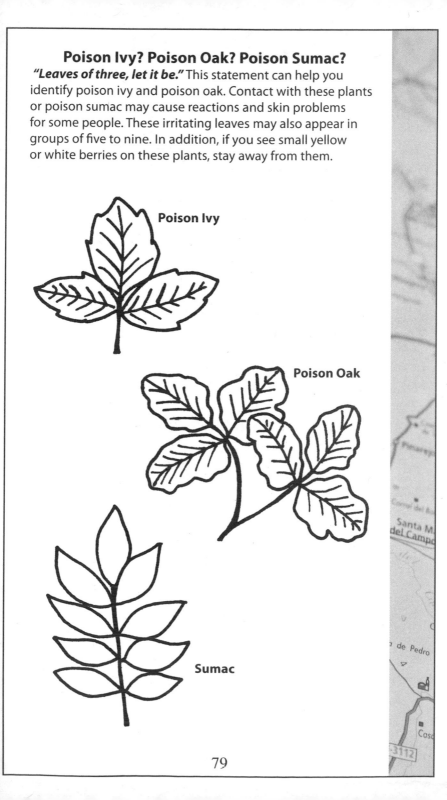

Poison Ivy

Poison Oak

Sumac

Placing Caches or Letterboxes Correctly

- Ask permission from a landowner (or managing agency) before you hide a cache.

- Do not hide a cache in any area where foot traffic could harm nature or the treasure hunters. This would include areas with rare or poisonous plants, endangered species or unstable ground.

- Label each cache or letterbox so others will know what they have found or stumbled across.

Creating Safe Caches and Letterboxes

- Everything you hide in a cache should be safe enough for a child to find. That means you should never place anything that is illegal, hazardous or of questionable moral value.

- Monitor the cache or letterbox regularly to assure the contents are still in good shape, the container is still hidden and there hasn't been any environmental damage.

Cache In, Trash Out (or Box In, Bag Out)

- Be a friend to nature. Bring a small trash bag along on your hike and pick up any trash you find along the way. Carry it out with you and discard it properly.

Don't Forget Your Stuff!

- Before leaving the site of your find, check to be sure you've gathered all your "stuff." Otherwise, it could be a frustrating hike back to retrieve your sunglasses, walking stick or GPSr.

Courtesies while Treasure Hunting

- To avoid compromising a cache or letterbox, don't handle food right before handling the treasures. This could attract animals that might destroy the cache later.

- Don't change the hiding spot or style of the cache or letterbox when you are putting it back after your find. It's alright to hide it a little better if it was too exposed, but keep it as the owner intended.

- Don't spoil the hunt for others. If you post your find online, don't share details that might give away the location of the treasure. And don't post pictures of the stamps you find because that also ruins the find for others.

- If you take a trinket from a geocache, leave another one of equal or greater value. "Trading up" is always a good idea (leaving something better than what you took).

- If you choose to take a travel bug or hitchhiker for a ride, be expedient. Do not keep the item at home for months before you move it to another spot. If you can't move it within a reasonably short period of time (within a month or so), let someone else take and move it.

FAQs

Q: *What if I find a cache or box that has been damaged?*

A: If the damage is something simple, like a leaking plastic bag or a missing pencil, you may want to replace those items for the owner. Some hikers carry extra supplies with them when they are hiking, just for this purpose. If the damage is more significant, you should report it on the website so the owner can fix, replace or remove it.

Q: *What if I meet other geocachers or letterboxers on the trail?*

A: It is alright to talk about the weather. It is alright to stamp each other's books if you're both agreeable, especially if you're carrying a "traveler" stamp. It is not alright to tell the other treasure hunter any clues or provide directions to finding the cache or letterbox.

Q: *If I find a cache and there are lots of people around, what should I do?*

A: Since there is an element of secrecy with any treasure hunt, it is best to discreetly remove the cache and carry it to a more private area where you can examine the contents and sign the log. This prevents disclosing the location to other hunters and ruining the hunt for them.

FAQs

Q: What if I can't find the cache or box where it was supposed to be?

A: There are several ways to handle this. You can come back another day to search and again enter the coordinates for a fresh reading. If you really feel that the treasure is missing or the coordinates are bad, report it online so the owner can check on it. Then watch the website for an update on this cache. If it is still hidden, you may be given other clues to help you find it. If it has gone missing, the owner should disable it on the website until it can be replaced, or if it won't be replaced, the cache or box should be retired.

Q: How do I choose the right container size for hiding a cache or letterbox?

A: Choose the smallest and sturdiest container that is large enough to hold the treasures you wish to enclose. By using a small container, you will have more and better choices of hiding spots and fewer accidental discoveries by non-players.

Q: If I cannot use a magnet, is there a way to hide and attach a micro to a non-metal surface?

A: Hook and loop Velcro strips can be used for this purpose. Purchase waterproof self-adhesive Velcro strips that are 2 inches wide. The adhesive side of the fuzzy section can be wrapped around the micro container. Press the adhesive of the Velcro's hooked side (stiffer section) to the clean surface of the place you wish to attach the micro. Press the Velcro-wrapped micro in place.

FAQs

Q: What should I do if I find a geocoin?

A: An official geocoin is activated online and has a tracking ID (usually a number and letter combination) so it can travel between geocaches and be followed through online log entries. If you find one, you can either leave it or take it. If you take it, visit the website listed on the geocoin and log your find. Then follow the instructions given by the coin's owner so the game can continue as s/he planned. Some coins are meant to be traded and collected, but you should not sell a geocoin that doesn't belong to you.

Geocoin by merkman, produced by Personal Geocoins.

Q: What is an event cache?

A: It is like a geocaching party. It offers a chance for geocachers to get together socially and talk about their hobby. A location is chosen, and the coordinates are saved and posted online with a date and time for the event. Then on the appointed date and time, geocachers follow the posted coordinates to find the party's location. Event caches are a good way to meet other people who share a passion for this sport.

Q: I sometimes lose track of counting paces. Is there an easy way to keep track of pacing distances besides counting?

A: Yes. A handheld punch counter or "pace beads" can help. To use pace beads, slide 1 bead over a string after a set number of paces. Then count the beads to figure out how far you've walked.

Let the
FUN & GAMES
Begin!

Try these games and stamping techniques,
then search online for other fun activities.

Geocaching Games

(These can be adapted for letterboxing, too.)

Hotter-Colder: A game of hints

Like the traditional Hot-Cold game, this is a great geocaching game for young children. If adults spot the hidden cache first, they shouldn't give it away. Keep the location a secret so the children can enjoy finding it on their own, too. Just give them hints as they walk either toward or away from the cache. "You're getting hotter" means the child is getting closer to the cache. "You're getting colder" (or in some cases, freezing!) means the child is moving farther away from the cache. When s/he is nearly on top of the cache, the chant becomes, "You're almost burning!"

Huckle-Buckle-Beanstalk: A game for a gang

When a group goes geocaching, this is a fun game to play. After one person finds the cache, s/he walks away without moving or opening the cache so the location isn't given away. Then s/he calls out the phrase "huckle-buckle-beanstalk" (or any other phrase the group wants to use). Everyone continues to look for the cache. The next person to find the cache does the same thing. This game continues until everyone in the group has spotted it or given up. Then the cache is uncovered for the whole group to look at and log.

Chicken: A hiking game

If your children quickly get tired of hiking and ask, "Are we there yet?", this is the game to play. Before your hike begins, enter the location of your starting point in your GPS receiver. Then choose a distance down the path that seems reasonable for your children, like a half mile or mile. Start walking and ask everyone to guess when they've walked that distance. Any player can yell "stop" when s/he thinks that distance has been reached. If you wish to keep score, give one point to the person who yelled "stop", only if the group has indeed walked that far. If stop was called before the distance was reached, give one point to every other player. Not only will this game help kids pass the time, it helps them learn to gauge distance.

It can also be played by a player stopping and then calling out the exact distance s/he thinks has been walked. Small prizes can be awarded to the player who is correct.

Hide-and-Seek: A people hunt

One person hides in a planned location or waypoint. Seekers must find the hidden person using their GPS receiver, as quickly as possible. The object of the game, of course, is to be the first person to find the hidden player.

Shutterspot: A photo game

Instead of using latitude and longitude coordinates to find a hidden object, you must look at an online photograph of an object or scene, and then search to find its exact location. You can find these photos in a specific region or city, or use other criteria to narrow your search area. After you think you've found the spot where the owner stood to take the photo, you record the latitude and longitude of that spot and then enter your guess online to see how close you were. For more information, go to an online search engine and type in "shutterspot".

Egg Hunt: A high-tech holiday game

Hide plastic Easter eggs and record the coordinates of each hidden egg with a GPS receiver. Divide your egg hunters into small groups and be sure each group has a GPS receiver to use. Give the list of coordinates to each group for a fun egg hunt using the technology of GPS receivers.

Benchmark Hunting: A surveying hunt

Long ago, when the United States was being plotted out, the National Coast and Geodetic Survey left permanent markers to assist future mapping and surveying tasks. Today, 700,000 location markers are listed in a database available for public use. Some geocachers like to hunt for these survey markers using the latitude and longitude coordinates listed in the database. On a search engine, type in "National Geodetic Survey Database" to search for markers in a specific county within a state. Some markers are brass or aluminum disks in the dirt; others are attached to concrete posts. These survey markers can also be natural permanent landmarks, such as mountain peaks, or tall manmade objects visible from a long distance away, such as water towers, fire lookout towers or church steeples.

Bingocaching: A numbers game

This is often an event game that is played in a small area, but it can also be a longer game meant to be played over time with caches hidden around an entire state. Players use a Bingo game board they get at an event or from a website. In each cache, a numbered token is hidden. When a player gets 5 correct numbers to make a Bingo, s/he calls it in to a game coordinator to check the answers. For longer games, the players can post their finds on the website instead.

Geko Smak: An imaginary lizards game

This game is made for Garmin-brand GPS receivers. The display screen shows a game board, but players actually play the game outside on a large field. When the screen shows a lizard popping up out of the ground, players must run to the correct location (following their GPSr) and press the OK button to "smack" the poor lizard before it disappears from the screen. Then another lizard pops up. These lizards show up faster and farther away as the game goes along. It's a great way to exercise and get a belly laugh at the same time.

Poker Run: An event game

This game is fun with a group of geocachers hunting in a specific area during a one- or two-day event. Clues are given to multiple caches and playing cards are hidden inside the caches. When players find each cache, they take a card from it to create their poker hand. When all the cards have been found, the player with the best 3-card poker hand wins a special prize. (The prizes may be items the players have put in as an ante before beginning the game.)

Story Cache: A writer's game

The owner of this cache writes the beginning of a story. Each hunter who finds this cache is supposed to creatively add text to the story. Who knows? In the end, it could be a great novel!

Geo-golf: A golfer's game

On a website, players choose and enter a starting point that is nearby and then let the computer generate 18 (or nine) random waypoints (holes) in that area. The object of this game is to go out looking for each of these waypoints, get as close to each one as possible and enter the coordinates. When the game is finished, the waypoints are entered on the website and it gives a score based on how close the player got to the assigned waypoints. The closer the player got to each point, the lower the score, and like golf, the lowest score wins. This can be played alone, in teams or against other players.

Capture the Flag: A team game

Divide a group of players into two teams. Each team needs one GPS receiver to use and one to hide. They may also want a strip of fabric or other "flag" to hide with the GPS receiver. Each team enters the latitude and longitude coordinates of a chosen "home base" into the GPS receiver they will hide with their flag. After hiding their items, each team must note the coordinates of the hiding spot. At the start of the game, each team gives the coordinates of its own hiding spot to the other team. Then Team A and Team B compete to find each other's GPSr and flag, look up the home base coordinates and return the items to the correct home base location first.

State Specialties: Games with local interest

Many states have special websites offering geocaching or letterboxing activities and tips to help people discover their scenic areas. Some states, like Utah, have special games unique to their state. One example is a game called "Are U Nuts". Nuts are hidden inside the caches, and geocachers are expected to move those nuts to a different cache within Utah to collect online points. A similar game, called "Just 4 Openers", asks geocachers to hide and collect colorful bottle caps. Go to an online search engine and type in "(your state's name) + geocaching" for an assortment of games and informational sites.

Games We've Played!

Game Name: _____

Date Played: _____

Results: _____

_____

Game Name: _____

Date Played: _____

Results: _____

_____

Game Name: _____

Date Played: _____

Results: _____

_____

Game Name: _____

Date Played: _____

Results: _____

_____

Game Name: _____

Date Played: _____

Results: _____

_____

Making Rubber Stamps
For Letterboxes

It's fun to make your own unique rubber stamp. The design you choose should be something that identifies you, like your signature. Do you have a favorite sport or hobby? Do you have a nickname that could be shown in a simple picture? If so, make your rubber stamp reflect that special quality about you. Follow the directions below to make your own rubber stamp.

To cut your own rubber stamp from an eraser you'll need:

    Art gum eraser, found at art, craft or discount stores
    Table knife
    Exacto knife (for adult use only)
    Optional tools: pencil, large paper clip, toothpick, small dowel

Directions

1. Draw or trace the desired shape on the large side of a gum eraser. Remember that the print will be backward from the design you carve. If you wish to have letters print correctly on paper, they must be drawn and cut in reverse on the eraser, like a mirror image. Although they will appear backward on the eraser, they will print correctly when stamped on paper.

2. Use the table knife to cut around the outer edges of the drawing by slicing through the eraser. You may cut all the way through or just partway through eraser and then slice it horizontally to remove small chunks.

3. Adult's job – Use an exacto knife to carve out small details by cutting about ½ inch deep into the eraser.

Other tools can be created and used to cut out stamp details as follows:

- Remove the small eraser on the top of a pencil with pliers and use the sharp metal edge on the pencil as a tool to cut out circles. Flatten the metal to use it as a carving tool.

- Straighten a paper clip and use one end to poke small holes into the eraser. Enlarge the holes as needed by pushing the clip in and out several times or pushing a toothpick, pencil point or dowel into the holes and turning it to "drill" out a small hole.

- Trace around the eraser on paper. Draw your sketch on the paper, making very heavy pencil lines. Set the plain side of eraser on top of the drawing, matching edges with the traced lines. Press down on the eraser until the pencil image shows on the eraser. This will be a mirror image. Cut out the design as directed above.

- Use novelty shaped erasers made for pencil toppers for perfect shapes. Carve out a small design from one side.

To use the stamp – Press the carved eraser firmly on an ink pad and coat the surface well. Press the inked side of the eraser stamp down evenly on paper. To add a round moon shape, dots or other round shape to your stamped image, press a pencil top eraser on the ink pad and stamp the circle imprint on the appropriate spot on your existing imprint.

To make your own rubber stamp from foam you'll need:
Craft foam
Wood block
Scissors
White glue
Optional: paper punch

Directions

1. Place the wood block on top of the foam piece and trace around it. Cut foam as traced.

2. Draw or trace a small shape on the foam piece. Cut out the shape.

3. If desired, use tiny scissors or paper punch to cut out any openings or details on the foam shape, such as eyes or stripes.

4. Glue the foam design to the flat side of the wood block. Let the glue dry completely.

To use stamp – Hold block and press the foam shape firmly on ink pad to coat the surface well. Press the inked side of the foam stamp down evenly on paper.

Stamp Patterns to Try

If desired, choose one of these designs to trace, then make your personal rubber stamp. Transfer the design to an eraser or foam piece as directed on pages 91 through 93. Carefully cut out the portions of the design you wish to remove, leaving the shapes intact that you wish to ink and print.

Stamps We've Made & Tried

Your
LOGBOOK PAGES

Use these pages as a beginning logbook. Fill in the blanks, sketch pictures or add photos you've taken to capture the memories from your outdoor adventures.

Logbook

Geocaching • Letterboxing *(Circle correct activity.)*

Date: _____

Today's hunt took us to _____

_____

_____

(Record the latitude and longitude, or the city or description of site.)

Here's what we found: _____

_____

_____

Memorable or funny moments: _____

_____

_____

For geocachers: Item(s) collected or exchanged: _____

_____

_____

For letterboxers: Rubber stamp found *(Stamp here.)*

Journaling

Logbook

Geocaching • Letterboxing *(Circle correct activity.)*

Date: _____

Today's hunt took us to _____

_____

_____

(Record the latitude and longitude, or the city or description of site.)

Here's what we found: _____

_____

_____

Memorable or funny moments: _____

_____

_____

For geocachers: Item(s) collected or exchanged: _____

_____

_____

For letterboxers: Rubber stamp found *(Stamp here.)*

Journaling

Logbook

Geocaching • Letterboxing *(Circle correct activity.)*

Date: _____

Today's hunt took us to _____

_____

_____

(Record the latitude and longitude, or the city or description of site.)

Here's what we found: _____

_____

_____

Memorable or funny moments: _____

_____

_____

For geocachers: Item(s) collected or exchanged: _____

_____

_____

For letterboxers: Rubber stamp found *(Stamp here.)*

Journaling

Logbook

Geocaching • Letterboxing *(Circle correct activity.)*

Date: _____

Today's hunt took us to _____

_____

_____

(Record the latitude and longitude, or the city or description of site.)

Here's what we found: _____

_____

_____

Memorable or funny moments: _____

_____

_____

For geocachers: Item(s) collected or exchanged: _____

_____

_____

For letterboxers: Rubber stamp found *(Stamp here.)*

Journaling

Logbook

Geocaching • Letterboxing *(Circle correct activity.)*

Date: _____

Today's hunt took us to _____

_____

_____

(Record the latitude and longitude, or the city or description of site.)

Here's what we found: _____

_____

_____

Memorable or funny moments: _____

_____

_____

For geocachers: Item(s) collected or exchanged: _____

_____

_____

For letterboxers: Rubber stamp found *(Stamp here.)*

Journaling

Logbook

Geocaching • Letterboxing *(Circle correct activity.)*

Date: _____

Today's hunt took us to _____

_____

_____

(Record the latitude and longitude, or the city or description of site.)

Here's what we found: _____

_____

_____

Memorable or funny moments: _____

_____

_____

For geocachers: Item(s) collected or exchanged: _____

_____

_____

For letterboxers: Rubber stamp found *(Stamp here.)*

Journaling

Logbook

Geocaching • Letterboxing *(Circle correct activity.)*

Date: _____

Today's hunt took us to _____

_____

_____

(Record the latitude and longitude, or the city or description of site.)

Here's what we found: _____

_____

_____

Memorable or funny moments: _____

_____

_____

For geocachers: Item(s) collected or exchanged: _____

_____

_____

For letterboxers: Rubber stamp found *(Stamp here.)*

Journaling

Logbook

Geocaching • Letterboxing *(Circle correct activity.)*

Date: _____

Today's hunt took us to _____

_____

_____

(Record the latitude and longitude, or the city or description of site.)

Here's what we found: _____

_____

_____

Memorable or funny moments: _____

_____

_____

For geocachers: Item(s) collected or exchanged: _____

_____

_____

For letterboxers: Rubber stamp found *(Stamp here.)*

Journaling

Logbook

Geocaching • Letterboxing *(Circle correct activity.)*

Date: _____

Today's hunt took us to _____

_____

_____

(Record the latitude and longitude, or the city or description of site.)

Here's what we found: _____

_____

_____

Memorable or funny moments: _____

_____

_____

For geocachers: Item(s) collected or exchanged: _____

_____

_____

For letterboxers: Rubber stamp found *(Stamp here.)*

Journaling

Logbook

Geocaching · Letterboxing *(Circle correct activity.)*

Date: _____

Today's hunt took us to _____

_____

_____

(Record the latitude and longitude, or the city or description of site.)

Here's what we found: _____

_____

_____

Memorable or funny moments: _____

_____

_____

For geocachers: Item(s) collected or exchanged: _____

_____

_____

For letterboxers: Rubber stamp found *(Stamp here.)*

Journaling

Logbook

Geocaching • Letterboxing *(Circle correct activity.)*

Date: _____

Today's hunt took us to _____

_____

_____

(Record the latitude and longitude, or the city or description of site.)

Here's what we found: _____

_____

_____

Memorable or funny moments: _____

_____

_____

For geocachers: Item(s) collected or exchanged: _____

_____

_____

For letterboxers: Rubber stamp found *(Stamp here.)*

Journaling

Glossary of Geocaching and Letterboxing Terms

Alphabet code – A way of cross-referencing letters to solve a code. The most common alphabet code used for geocaching is the Rot13 code.

Bearing – A direction that is measured in degrees on a compass and used while traveling to stay on course.

Cache *(pronounced kash or cash, as in money, and rhymes with flash)* – A hidden container with a logbook, pen or pencil and sometimes, trinkets for trading. Another word for a geocache.

CITO – Cache In, Trash Out. Hikers are encouraged to carry a bag along to pick up and dispose of trash while geocaching.

Clues – The descriptions, tips and hints provided online that are used to find geocaches and letterboxes.

Compass – A handheld navigational tool with a magnetic needle used by letterboxers and sometimes geocachers to determine which geographical direction to travel.

Datum – The system used for figuring out latitude and longitude; geocaching generally uses the WGS84 datum for caches so a GPS receiver should be set on this system.

E count – The number of stamp imprints collected at a letterboxing event.

Geobox – One name for a geocaching and letterboxing hybrid. See Hybrid.

Geocache – See Cache.

Geocoin (or geo-coin) – Small, custom-made and numbered coins that may be left inside geocaches for trading. They can be collected, traded and tracked online.

Geomuggles – Anyone who is not a geocacher, does not know about the sport or who accidentally finds a cache. (This term was adapted from the Harry Potter books.)

GeoStripes – Scratches on the arms and legs from geocaching adventures.

GPS receiver (GPSr) – A Global Positioning System unit that receives signals from satellites orbiting the earth and locks in the latitude and longitude coordinates of locations on the earth. Geocachers use a handheld receiver to find caches.

Hitchhiker – Trinkets or other items placed inside caches that are meant to be moved from one cache to another. Their travels are often tracked in an accompanying logbook and online entries.

Hybrid – A combination of geocaching and letterboxing activities. The container holds a rubber stamp and logbook (like letterboxing) plus clues that require the use of a GPS receiver (like geocaching). There may be letterboxing riddles and geocaching trinkets to exchange. Also known as Geobox or Lettercache.

Letterbox – A hidden container with a logbook and special rubber stamp inside.

Lettercache – One name for a letterboxing and geocaching hybrid. See Hybrid.

Log – Another name for logbook. (When used as a verb, it means to record an entry in a logbook.)

Logbook – Paper, usually in the form of a small notebook or unlined sketchbook. Each geocache and letterbox includes a small logbook for visitors to sign and many hobbyists carry a personal logbook with them to record finds and experiences.

Latitude and Longitude coordinates – The world's navigation system to measure distances on the earth based on a globe. For geocaching, the distances are measured in degrees and decimal minutes. Latitude lines are horizontal; they measure north and south coordinates. Longitude lines are vertical; they measure east and west coordinates. When a set of coordinates is entered into a GPS receiver, it can calculate distances correctly. A pair of latitude and longitude coordinates is called a Waypoint.

Micros (geocaches or letterboxes) – The tiniest caches or letterboxes.

Muggles – See Geomuggles.

PF count – When a letterboxer counts how many boxes s/he has planted (P) and found (F).

Plant – A letterboxing term for placing or hiding a letterbox.

Post – Writing an entry to be displayed on a website. It might be a summary of an adventure or a description of a treasure you have hidden.

Rot13 code – A way to encrypt a clue or hint for finding a geocache using the alphabet.

Signature item – A personalized trinket or phrase left by a geocacher each time that identifies him/her in some way.

Signature stamp – The rubber stamp left inside a letterbox which becomes the "signature" of that box. It also refers to the personal stamp carried by each letterboxer to stamp in or "sign" logbooks.

Social trail – A path that is created when lots of people walk toward a cache or letterbox. This trail can give away the secret location of the hidden treasure.

Spoiler – A person or information that tells too many details and gives away or spoils a hunt for someone else.

Stamping in – After finding a letterbox, using your personal rubber stamp to make an inked imprint of it in the letterbox's logbook.

Stash – Another word for a cache and its contents. Geocaching was originally called the "Great American GPS Stash Hunt".

Swag – The trinkets in a geocache.

Trail name – A nickname used to sign logbooks and website entries.

Traveler – A second rubber stamp that serious letterboxers carry in case they meet another letterboxer during a hunt. The two letterboxers can exchange traveler stamp imprints without giving away their signature stamp.

Waypoint – A particular location that can be entered as a set of coordinates on a GPS receiver, stored and recalled as needed. It may be the cache location itself or other spots along the way.

WoM clues – Word of mouth clues. These clues are shared verbally but not online.

X count – The number of stamp imprints personally exchanged with other letterboxers.

Index

Index

Index